BROKEN EARS, WOUNDED HEARTS

BROKEN EARS, WOUNDED HEARTS

George A. Harris

Gallaudet College Press
Washington, D.C.

Published 1983 by the Gallaudet College Press
Kendall Green, Washington, DC 20002

Family members and friends retain their real names in this book. Other given names and surnames have been changed where necessary to protect confidentiality or identity. Any resemblance between the fictional names and people associated with institutions described herein is purely coincidental.

Printed in the United States of America

Gallaudet College is an equal opportunity employer/educational institution. Programs and services offered by Gallaudet College receive substantial financial support from the U.S. Department of Education.

Library of Congress Cataloging in Publication Data

Harris, George A., 1950-
  Broken ears, wounded hearts.

  1. Harris, Jennifer, 1969–   . 2. Children, Deaf—United States—Biography. 3. Children, Deaf—United States—Family relationships.
I. Title.
HV2534.H33H37 1983   362.8'2[B]   82-21044

ISBN 0-913580-83-X

To Jennifer, of course

I could have a different slant on things, perhaps, if I were not living in this inconsolable loneliness. And that is an insoluble problem. I mean, you could go up to a stranger on the street and say, "I am inconsolably lonely," and he might take you home with him and introduce you to his family and ask you to stay for dinner. But that wouldn't help. Because loneliness is not a longing for company, it is a longing for kind. And kind means people who can see you for who you are, and that means they have enough intelligence and sensitivity and patience to do that.

Marilyn French
The Women's Room

All parents experience a wide range of feelings with the discovery that one of their children has a severe handicap. The joy and hope that the birth of a healthy, normal baby brings into a family is rudely replaced by grief, worry, and despair. We all hope and pray that our children will be normal. When this is not the case, we feel cheated and angry. With time these feelings subside; but they may well up again when a school seems unresponsive to our requests or our child faces some insurmountable hurdle that normal children scale with ease.

Guilt and despair can drain us of needed energy. Anger can smolder for months, then flare up at a spouse — even at the child we love and want to help. How do parents solve these problems? How do they recapture the joy and hope that accompanied the birth of their baby? How do they develop and maintain the necessary assertiveness to demand appropriate services for their growing child? *Broken Ears, Wounded Hearts* is a touching, instructive story that speaks to these questions.

There are two stories that thread their way through this book. One is about the persistent search by a young couple to discover what is wrong with their infant daughter. This is an absorbing story, full of suspense and surprise, humor and dismay, emotion and drama. From the moment of Jennifer's premature birth, her parents must make crucial medical decisions affecting their daughter's very life. Their pursuit of an accurate diagnosis of Jennifer's mental and auditory capabilities forces both parents to weigh their observations against those of professionals. When the professionals disagree, the parents seek other opinions or ferret out more appropriate school programs for their daughter. All readers can benefit from their example of persistence.

There is a second and more important story here: what Jennifer did for her parents. Like anyone struck by personal tragedy, Jennifer's parents wonder why this happened to them. Why must their daughter begin life with so many handicaps? They struggle with their guilt, and they blame each other for their unfortunate circumstances. Communication becomes almost as difficult for them as it is for their strangely silent daughter. Yet, in the face of all these difficulties, the love their daughter stirs up within them provides the strength to cooperate for her benefit.

This is a story I personally enjoyed reading. But it is more than just a good story. Here is the opportunity for all readers to experience the raw emotions that grip parents facing similar circumstances. Here is the chance for these parents to understand that such feelings are normal. Here is the occasion to learn why parents must sometimes resort to legal procedures to get their children placed in appropriate school programs.

To read this book is to experience the joy of knowing a young girl, different in many ways but no less human; for parents it is an invitation to look at their own children through new eyes and to recapture, if need be, the joy and hope lost in earlier years.

Broken Ears, Wounded Hearts is written for everyone, but parents and professionals involved with handicapped children should not fail to read it. The intensity of the author's emotions may shock some parents. His frankness may offend some professionals. For better or for worse, both parents and professionals are likely to see themselves in the pages of this story.

For anyone who provides services to parents or their handicapped children, here is the opportunity to gain insight and experience personal growth. For parents who still carry the sorrow of wounded hearts, here is the opportunity to let the healing process begin.

Thomas S. Spradley
Co-author, *Deaf Like Me*

ACKNOWLEDGMENTS

My thanks to the following: Virginia Pruitt, who expertly
advised me on an early draft of the book; Audrey Bolton
who patiently typed and retyped revisions; Jim Stentzel at
Gallaudet College Press for his thoughtful, caring attention to the changes needed to express the experience
accurately; Marilyn French, author of *The Women's
Room,* for permission to quote her; and Rainelle, whose
love for Jennifer is so much more evident to me as time
passes.

CHAPTER 1

Present Illness: This 1,410 gram premature Caucasian girl was born at approximately 30 weeks gestation to a 19 year old gravida I, para I, pre-eclamptic female. The delivery was sterile, vaginal, controlled, spontaneous, without complications. The patient did not breathe spontaneously. She had an Apgar of 7 at 1 minute and 9 at 5 minutes. With physical stimulation and oxygen the patient showed improved respiratory effort and seemed to do better.
— Medical Report, December 2, 1969, Columbia, Missouri

The day had been cold, and the night was colder. The small oil furnace in our trailer made a low rumbling sound as it struggled to keep us warm. My wife and I were comfortable, nestled in our little cocoon, so long as the electrical heat tape kept the water pipes from freezing and the furnace kept working. The trailer was small—just big enough for a couch, refrigerator, oven, bed, and bathroom. It was not actually a mobile home but a travel trailer. I could walk without ducking every place except the bathroom, where I had to crouch. Situated next to a creek levee, the trailer was bright and cheerful on the inside. Though the trailer court was a bit dumpy, we enjoyed the creek and the trees and shrubs of the valley where the trailer was parked.

One of my friends came to visit my wife and me. Cameron and I always got along well, perhaps because we were from the same hometown, which gave us the opportunity to talk about people we knew. I was usually considered pretty "straight," but my friends weren't; Cameron, the first person I ever heard say "hassle," was no exception. Both of us were going to college, but he seemed to be more into the college life than I was.

He and I were playing chess. That's about all we could do in the trailer; there wasn't room to do anything else. I noticed Rainelle making frequent trips to the bathroom but thought nothing of it at the time. Later I guessed she had been too embarrassed to say anything in front of Cameron. Or being nineteen (like myself) and pregnant, she may have been frightened or confused. Her water had burst, but she said later she didn't know for sure what that meant. When Cameron left, she said she thought she'd better call the hospital, which was just a few blocks away. She did, and the nurse said the baby was on its way. It was two months early.

We piled into our old beat-up Mustang with rusted rocker panels and hard-to-start engine and drove to the hospital.

I can't remember all that occurred except that I spent most of the night in the hospital lobby, curled up by the forced air heater that comforted me with its steady warmth. I stayed with Rainelle in the labor room for a while, but later this wasn't allowed.

I really didn't have any friends I wanted to call. My parents were 150 miles away, and I didn't want to call them either. I didn't understand what was happening, but it didn't seem as though anyone could really help.

As I sat in the hospital lobby, my thoughts drifted off to earlier times. I saw Rainelle in the beige dress she was wearing when we first met. Her long slender legs supported her gracefully. A purple silk scarf was wrapped around her neck, just below the line of her short dark hair. On our first date we went to a basketball game at my high school.

2

I was proud to be seen with her. She was pretty, and she was unknown to my friends because she went to a different school. In my memory I saw her sitting in the bleachers, politely cheering for my team.

My thoughts stopped wandering when I noticed a man, head in hands, on the other side of the lobby. I wondered if he too was reflecting on other times.

It was difficult to get anyone to answer questions about my wife's condition. My queries were met with polite but reserved responses. I spent most of the night in the hospital alone, not knowing why I couldn't be in the labor room with Rainelle. Finally, someone approached me.

"Congratulations, Mr. Harris, you have a daughter, three pounds and two ounces. You can see your wife in a while." At the time it was probably just as well that no one explained the potentially fatal blood pressure complications that Rainelle had encountered.

Jennifer, our daughter, was placed in an incubator. Rainelle and I were allowed to see Jennifer the next day when the nurses wheeled her up to the plate glass window that separated the "preemie" ward and its incubators from the parents. Plastic tubes seemed to be coming out of every orifice on her body. She was so tiny that I could have held her in one hand.

"When can she come home?" I asked.

"Well," the resident doctor replied, "she has some problems we need to see about, and she has to gain some weight."

"Oh," we said, deflated. We didn't ask what problems.

"She looks like you, Mr. Harris," the doctor said. I stared at him until I decided he was just trying to be nice.

Rainelle was allowed to come home two or three days later. We began to establish a visitation ritual. Every afternoon and evening we went to the hospital for the plate glass special. Jennifer's incubator was rolled up to the window. We noticed what new tubes were inserted or old ones removed; no one ever told us why.

"How many ounces has she gained?" we always asked.

"One-half ounce. That's good," the nurse might answer,

and we cheered. Or, "She's lost a little, but that's to be expected," the nurse would say, and we just stood there not knowing what to do.

Usually the parents of another preemie would show up, and we would ask about their baby's condition before we left the viewing window. It was all very awkward. The healthy babies' window was on the way out, and occasionally we would stop to view them in their bassinets. We never spoke about the jealousy we felt for the parents of these kids, and certainly not about the anger I felt but didn't recognize at the time: Why wasn't our baby normal! How had this happened!

At Christmas Rainelle and I visited our parents and hometowns, where everyone knows everything already but inquires about it all the same. I suppose everyone was well-intentioned, but the social exchanges were embarrassing.

"Hi, George. How's the baby?" friends would ask.

"Oh, okay. She's gaining weight," I would answer, failing to add that at the current rate it would take a year before she was as big as most babies at birth. Jennifer's progress was slow. She seemed little more than three pounds of wrinkled flesh.

Some acquaintances advised us not to let the "minor" problems with this child scare us away from having other children. Other friends didn't realize how sick I was of listening to stories about other premature children who "grew up to be just fine."

I didn't realize how angry I was about the whole thing until one day a card arrived in the mail from a state representative wishing us happiness with our newborn child. I wrote back scathingly that I would be quite happy if she just lived and if he would quit doing public relations on state stationery. His response, on state letterhead, was apologetic.

The days blended into each other. One day it dawned on me that my student insurance might not pay for Jennifer's treatment. There still was no date in sight for Jennifer to come home. I was only an observer to all the medical miracles going on behind that plate glass. For all I knew I would be paying the bill for the rest of my life. There wasn't much that could be done about this; I decided just to wait to see what would happen.

There were lighter moments in all this. For example, Rainelle and I discovered that the elevators in the hospital really picked up speed if they didn't have to stop between the ground floor and the tenth floor preemie ward. So when we came to the hospital, we loitered around the elevators until we got one by ourselves. Quickly we closed the doors so no one could interfere with our fun, and off we went on our carnival ride. As the elevator picked up speed we watched the lights indicating what floors we were passing. As the tenth floor neared, we crouched slightly; at the last moment, like olympic ski-jumpers, we timed our leap to coincide with the elevator's rapid stop. The elevator floor seemed to drop out from beneath us as the momentum plus our jump lifted us high above the now motionless elevator floor. We landed with a thump, thump. The elevator door opened to reveal two giggling teenagers going to see their baby.

One day Jennifer's physician took us aside. He explained that Jennifer's heart was having to pump overtime to get enough blood to the right places. The doctor drew a diagram to explain the surgical procedure she needed, but I couldn't pay much attention. My mind was wandering, scattered in a thousand confused directions.

Rainelle and I were gloomy as we left the nursery that day. Heart surgery seemed so awesome. We got on the elevator and plummeted with it to the lobby.

The day of the surgery arrived. The purpose of the surgery was to close off a tube that was allowing blood to bypass Jennifer's lungs. In normal births this happens automatically. In premature births the tube sometimes stays open. Though the doctors were optimistic, they weren't positive that the operation would be a success. Rainelle's mother and my parents drove two hours to the hospital, though I had told them there was nothing they could do there. We were all at the hospital, bumping into one another. I consciously reasoned that I might as well go to my classes since everything else to that point had been done without anyone filling me in beforehand. I felt so useless, and I wanted to escape.

Rainelle looked blankly at me when I said where I was going, but she said nothing.

Jennifer was being operated on at the University of Missouri Medical Center, so my classes were not far away. I stumbled into class, the sociology of class, status, and power, feeling rather removed from everything. The instructor droned on and on. When class was over I stumbled back to the hospital, feeling very powerless.

Jennifer was still in surgery. My relatives were sitting in the waiting room. The room was painted institutional green and seemed to make everyone appear flat and one-dimensional, like sad figures on a mural.

We waited.

We stared at each other.

We mumbled polite encouragements and platitudes until I wanted to scream.

"They'll probably be finished soon," said my mother-in-law, who worked in a hospital.

"It's in God's hands," my mother remarked.

I couldn't find words to say anything to Rainelle, whom I sat next to without touching. I was off in my own thoughts.

Finally, Jennifer's doctor came to say that the operation was a success. There was some other mention of her not being totally out of the woods, but this didn't seem important. We all smiled and went to lunch celebrating Jennifer's future.

We were in the middle of a Missouri winter. Jennifer, about six weeks old, had survived her surgery; I hoped I would survive the unusually bitter cold that kept freezing the water pipes in the trailer. Jennifer's weight gain continued to be slow. Rainelle and I visited the hospital regularly to watch Jennifer through the window.

The lights were on twenty-four hours a day in the preemie ward, and we wondered how this could affect Jennifer. How could she sleep with all that light! The nurses did put little masks around the infants' eyes, but this seemed so complicated. We wondered why they couldn't just dim the lights.

The nurses fondly nicknamed Jennifer "Pitiful Pearl" because of her scrawny appearance, and the name stuck.

After evening visitation Rainelle and I always climbed into our car and discussed the day's news. Five pounds had been set as the weight Jennifer needed to attain before she could come home. Rainelle was promised she could put on a gown and go in to hold Jennifer soon. She was excited and eager for the chance. We began to ask how many ounces of formula Jennifer consumed rather than just how much weight she gained. Every piece of information was precious. As we left the hospital parking lot we looked up to the tenth floor to see the light in the window of Jennifer's hospital home.

"Goodnight, pumpkin," we yelled.

"Sleep tight, Pitiful Pearl," we said, knowing she couldn't hear us but hoping she could feel our thoughts somehow.

Life during these months was confusing. On the one hand, I was a new father; but I felt embarrassed because Jennifer was so sickly, and I refused to allow pictures to be taken of the baby in the incubator. As a new father, I felt responsibility; but I had no resources to meet my responsibilities. I had no idea how the hospital bill, mounting daily, would be paid, or how baby clothes, crib, and food would be purchased. I was still a student, a sophomore at the University of Missouri. As my classmates raced from classes to fraternity parties and dates, I went to the hospital to see my baby. I had gotten events in the wrong order, and it was a mess.

At the time Rainelle learned she was pregnant, we had discussed how and whether each of us could finish our last three years of college if we got married and kept the baby. Neither of us had any substantial financial support from parents; loans and scholarships were all we had. It didn't take long to figure out that my financial aid alone wouldn't be enough, so Rainelle had to keep going to school too. Otherwise, I would have to quit and get a full-time job. We had figured that Jennifer would be born after the first semester ended. We hoped Rainelle would then be able to return to classes the second semester by resting up over Christmas break. We didn't plan on Jennifer's being premature.

I was able to make it through that first semester; but Rainelle's grades suffered. But we both enrolled for the winter semester.

Jennifer's weight gain was still slow, but by the end of February she was approaching five pounds. One day when I came home, Rainelle met me at the door of our trailer.

"Jennifer's coming home!" she shrieked.

I didn't have time to blink before I was lugging to the car what seemed like thirty pounds of blankets, bonnets, diapers, and other assorted baby clothes.

We drove to the hospital where I, for the first time in three months, got to touch my child. Rainelle had been allowed to hold and rock Jennifer a few times. She already loved our little girl in a way I did not understand.

Hospital Records: February 9, 1970
Jennifer Harris, DOB 12/2/69

Discharge Diagnosis:
1. Prematurity by weight and date
2. Congenital heart disease, patent ductus ateriosus, probable septal defect

3. Congestive heart failure
4. Pulmonary hypertension
5. Sepsis
6. Thrombocytopenia

Operations and Treatments:
1. Ligation of patent ductus arteriosus

Disposition:
The patient was discharged to continue taking Digoxin 0.015 mg. (0.3cc) q12h, and Diuril suspension 0.5cc b.i.d., q.i.d. She was to continue taking her formula 40cc every 2 hours and to include Tri-vi-sol and Fer-in-sol. The patient was given a return to the clinic in two weeks.

Holding Jennifer was an awkward experience for me; she was so tiny. Many people remarked that she looked like me, but I couldn't see the resemblance. Besides, Rainelle usually wrapped her in so many blankets that only her face showed, making it hard to tell what she really did look like. Typical mother, I supposed. Love for a child might be proportional to the number of blankets wrapped around it, like the number of rings denotes the age of a tree.

Our trailer was eight feet wide and twenty-eight feet long. There was no extra bedroom, so Jennifer took up residence in a borrowed crib placed near the front door. A mobile with a music box and plastic elephants dangling from strings was attached to the head of the crib, but Jennifer paid this little attention.

Because of Jennifer's heart problem, medicine was prescribed which we were to give her orally. The green syrup had to be administered by sucking up about a teaspoonful in a syringe then slowly releasing it into Jennifer's mouth, taking care not to release too much too fast which would cause her to choke. Sometimes Jennifer simply closed her lips and the medicine dribbled messily off her cheek. We had to push the corners of her lips, forcing her mouth open wide enough to create a small pocket for the medicine.

Like most new babies, Jennifer's sleeping habits were not regular. Though I had always been a heavy sleeper,

9

for some reason I awoke whenever Jennifer so much as stirred. It seemed sensible, then, for me to get up to feed and give Jennifer her medicine. Another factor was that Rainelle slept on the side of the bed next to the wall because a cabinet at the foot of the bed prevented my long legs from dangling over the end. She would have had to crawl over me to get out of bed. So I took responsibility for Jennifer at night. Because Rainelle handled most of the daytime chores, this seemed a fair arrangement. I did feel irritated, however, when Rainelle slept through Jennifer's nighttime crying. At least she could wake up and watch, I thought. Now I wish I had known how to ask for help.

I chuckled to myself thinking of Jennifer as my Dr. Pepper girl; I could depend on her being up at 10, 2, and 4...and then some. Many nights as I fed Jennifer I sat on the couch by her crib, listening to the winter wind, gazing into the darkness outside, wondering about her future.

In hospital lingo, Jennifer was "given a return" to the hospital well-baby clinic for checkups. My student status and poverty level placed us in a charity category, so most of the fees for the clinic were waived, thank goodness. I learned that Jennifer's original hospital bill was $3,500.00, just about the amount of money we lived on in 1969. I worried myself sick for weeks until the hospital finally told me the charges had been waived. I didn't know how to share my worry with Rainelle, and I didn't give her credit for being able to shoulder the burden with me.

The nurses at the clinic did their usual measuring of temperature, weight, and length. Then the medical students came in to check Jennifer. They all seemed to spend a lot of time listening to her heart. After the students finished, their supervisor arrived to check the findings by repeating all the steps the students had just performed. This was all very slow and boring, but, then, the price was right.

One day during a checkup, surrounded by a lot of unintelligible talk between students and supervisor, I overheard a comment about a murmur.

"What does this murmur thing mean?" I interrupted.

"Uh, well, she has a little extra sound in her heart," her doctor said.

"Is that serious?"

"Well, uh, didn't you know that Jennifer probably has, uh, a hole between two chambers?" he asked.

Flashes of conversations poured through my head... "not out of the woods"... "septal defect." Crestfallen, we asked for details.

The doctor explained that the defect was probably small because it made a loud noise, like water rushing through a tiny hose. No, they weren't sure where it was. No, they didn't know if they would have to operate again. No, she wasn't in immediate danger. No, her growth wasn't slow because of this problem.

We finished the examination and returned home to eat dinner in silence.

We watched Jennifer closely after learning of her heart problem. We had been assured she would not have a heart failure, turn blue, or act strange. But we watched anyway. She cried and defecated like every baby, but she did not seem to take interest in things around her. Of course, she was still tiny and couldn't even lift her head without help. I didn't expect her to get up and turn on the news, so nothing seemed abnormal. Sometimes she would wake up when Rainelle dropped a pan on the stove; other times, even when she was wide awake, similar loud noises didn't make her blink. But she was still little, after all.

Rainelle and I tried to juggle our school schedules so we could both attend classes but at different times. It was a nice idea which worked until Jennifer came home from the hospital; then Rainelle often had to skip classes. I was working part-time washing live frogs to prepare them for the ritual slaughter called Biology 101. With my classes, studying, and work, everything was pretty hectic.

Spring in Missouri is usually pretty but wet. As the rains fell, the creek behind our trailer rose. Rainelle and I periodically checked the creek. It scared me, but Rainelle didn't seem worried. One night the water was perilously close to topping the levee. I decided that a mobile home should be mobile, so I hired a truck to move it to higher ground. Rainelle, loaded with diapers and formula, went with Jennifer to Cameron's apartment.

The trailer was saved, but the next several days were washed out as far as attending classes. Rainelle just seemed to lose interest in school after that. With all the schedule juggling, Rainelle had not gotten to take the courses she wanted anyway. She told me later she felt I had made my schedule a priority over hers, and she resented my lack of consideration.

During the summer, my parents offered to lend me money to buy a bigger trailer, and I accepted. My brother took the travel trailer, lived in it for a few months, and eventually sold it to some gypsies. Actually, they just worked for a carnival, but "gypsies" sounded more interesting when telling the story to friends. We moved into our spacious new home, all five hundred square feet. Jennifer had her own room and seemed unperturbed by the move. In fact, she seemed oblivious to the move, sleeping through all the commotion of dropped furniture and clatter of jars and glassware.

It was quite a relief to have more space. Also, after the flood, the levee was raised several feet, so everything seemed secure.

A new school year was about to begin. Rainelle had been put on academic probation, but school officials were going to allow her to continue. The financial aids office had taken away one of my scholarships because my grades had dropped, but I talked them into giving me a loan. With a sigh of relief, we forged ahead.

Our new trailer sat next to a road. One afternoon an ambulance careened down the road with siren blaring. Reflexively, Rainelle and I both covered our ears, but Jennifer didn't stir. Rainelle commented that Jennifer didn't seem to be bothered by loud noises.

"She's still young," I said. "She'll pay more attention later."

"I don't know. Watch this," Rainelle said as she clapped her hands behind Jennifer. Jennifer didn't move.

Another ambulance raced by, siren wailing; this time Jennifer started to cry. Rainelle looked at me, puzzled. Our amateur audiology had proved nothing.

"Maybe we ought to have her examined," Rainelle mused out loud, and I agreed. We never articulated our suspicions that Jennifer was deaf.

On our next visit to the well-baby clinic we asked the doctors and almost doctors about Jennifer's hearing. They referred us to the Missouri School for the Deaf in Fulton for an audiological examination.

Rainelle took Jennifer for the exam and came home depressed.

Jennifer was deaf.

"What did they say caused it?" I wanted to know.

"They don't know," Rainelle said.

"Is she totally deaf?" I asked.

"They're not sure. They said she's too small to get good results," Rainelle said.

"What do we do now?" I asked, my logical mind still in control of my gut feelings.

Rainelle said that the audiologist had referred us to a speech therapist at the University Medical Center. The therapist would teach us how to work with Jennifer to make the most out of whatever hearing she still had.

That evening Jennifer blinked when I yelled behind her crib. Maybe, we thought, she had some hearing.

Relatives' reactions to the news were varied. Rainelle's mother instantly recalled a deaf relative. Almost everyone remembered a time when Jennifer had turned her head toward a loud noise. My mother reasoned that the problem with Jennifer's heart was probably keeping the blood from circulating properly and that, when this problem was fixed, Jennifer's hearing would return.

We began speech therapy training. The teacher, Miss Green, came to our trailer one evening and introduced herself. She was dressed neatly, almost primly. I wondered if she would come within a yard of a baby in wet diapers. She didn't. Most memorable was that someone had painted a smile on teacher, a smile so stiff I wondered if she would keep the same expression for the whole hour. She did.

But she was a good teacher. The purpose of our work was to learn how to train Jennifer to respond to sound of any kind. Miss Green instructed us to get a big metal pot and a wooden spoon. Then, while Rainelle propped Jennifer up in the middle of the floor and played with her, I was to sneak behind Jennifer and bang the pot loudly. If Jennifer oriented to the sound at all, we were supposed to smile and pat her enthusiastically to let her know she should continue to do that.

The pot soon had dents all over, but Jennifer didn't respond.

"Don't worry," said Miss Green. She showed us some words to try to teach Jennifer to lipread. "Repetition is the key," she said.

We proceeded to spend an hour each day crouching down at Jennifer's level when we talked. In this way she could see our mouths move and begin to learn lipreading—just in case she really was deaf.

Our lessons with Jennifer continued as Christmas of 1970 approached. Though one year old, Jennifer was not yet sleeping regularly. She still was unable even to sit up by herself. But one week before Christmas she pushed and twisted and finally moved her frail little body upright. She wobbled, but she did it.

I reasoned that Jennifer was really only nine months old; the first two or three months of her life shouldn't count because of her prematurity, and therefore she wasn't lagging in her development nearly as much as she seemed to be. Jennifer just needed time to catch up and she would be all right; she was making progress.

My mind's eye still sees our trailer sitting in the low-lying seedy little trailer court at the foot of a small hill next to a creek. When I would enter the driveway in the evening, the kitchen lights would beckon through windows fogged over from dinner cooking on the stove, and I would look forward to a warm and cozy evening.

But the pleasant anticipation of dinner sometimes didn't seem to be enough to sustain the mood through the evening. Rainelle was enrolled primarily in evening classes, but either I would come home too late for her to get ready or she would just decide not to go. Rainelle didn't have a driver's license, so she couldn't drive herself. My irritation about having to drive her to school showed regularly.

"So what am I, your chauffeur?" I yelled.

Rainelle cried and turned away. This was a pattern of hers, one which barely concealed her anger at me. She said later that she really felt like hitting me.

Jennifer also seemed increasingly irritable, crying for hours on end. I questioned whether Rainelle was feeding her properly during the day. "She's not gaining weight like she should. Are you feeding her right?" I demanded.

We managed to live through these nights; there wasn't any choice. Our life, like the creek that ran by our trailer court, was only intermittently turbulent.

While we were trying to get Jennifer to respond to sounds, we were also trying to get her to eat and drink like a child should.

[Diary, March 1971]

I never thought how hard it would be to describe to a child how to suck through a straw. You don't explain how; you can demonstrate, but demonstration really only shows the straw changing color as the liquid goes up. You might combine demonstration with explanation or description. You could say, "Watch, see how the Coke goes up the straw as I suck on it? (slurp) See how I did that? You do it." And if the person you were talking to knew what "suck" meant (aren't all humans born with the ability to suck?) then you'd be off and running.

The problem is, what if you're trying to teach someone who can't talk or who has no language? Then things get more difficult. Perhaps Jennifer was born without innate

15

sucking reflexes. When she came home from the hospital, she required hours to suckle a few ounces of milk. Sometimes I think that gravity was the only thing that saved her, by forcing out drops for her to swallow.

As she got older and stronger and learned to drink from a cup, she developed a fondness for Coke. (Even learning to drink from a cup was tough. First, Jennifer had to use the Tommee Tippee cup which was a cross between a nipple and a cup, with a spout for the child to wrap her mouth around, but the cup was otherwise sealed.) In any event, it was Coke that finally motivated Jennifer to drink from a straw because, when we would go to a drive-in restaurant, she knew that the paper cup with lid and straw held Coke. When she was given the cup, she would tilt it, scratch it, shake it, and cry at it—everything but suck on the straw in it. Rainelle and I were as frustrated trying to teach Jennifer to suck as Jennifer was trying to learn.

We sat in the car pursing our lips and sucking in our cheeks, but it was hard to get her to watch us. Her concentration was on the cup, and her frustration level was low. We would exaggerate the demonstration to grab Jennifer's attention, hoping she would see something and respond. I can only imagine what passers-by must have thought as they watched two parents sucking on imaginary straws as baby held the cup. It was, I'm sure, a strange sight.

Jennifer was so impulsive that it was hard to keep her from pulling the lid off the cup and drinking as she did at home. As soon as we stopped her from trying to remove the lid, she would try it again. I wished often for extra arms.

After a time, Jennifer got the idea of pursing her lips around the straw, and she learned to suck weakly after we demonstrated sucking by sucking on her finger. However, she didn't quite understand why it was necessary to seal her lips around the straw. She would suck and suck and get only air. Rainelle and I would try to push her little lips around the straw. Jennifer always looked confused and annoyed.

For a time, Jennifer mauled straws in her attempts to learn the knack. When I asked for a half-dozen extra straws, the drive-in cashiers usually complied, sometimes skeptically.

Jennifer practiced and practiced and finally began to get the Coke to pop up the straw almost to her mouth. We applauded enthusiastically each time she got close to tasting the Coke, but the precious drink always fell disappointingly back into the cup.

Finally, Rainelle got a brilliant idea. Jennifer was able to suck the Coke halfway up the straw so if we cut the straw in half, maybe she could get a little taste, which would reward her for her efforts. The trick worked. The look of delight and surprise in Jennifer's eyes when she finally succeeded was worth all the effort.

There was a problem left to be solved, however. Jennifer couldn't quite figure out how to get the straw out of her mouth without losing the Coke she had collected. She dribbled Coke messily for several weeks before she learned to close her lips as she withdrew the straw to swallow. But this problem was eventually solved. She even learned how to get the plastic lid off the cup to get to the ice and eat it. . . just like I do.

CHAPTER 2

Another Missouri winter was coming to an end. We had given up banging on pots around Jennifer because she didn't seem to be paying any attention. Sometimes she seemed to turn when we talked to her, and we wondered if her hearing might be sporadic or if she was just playing games with us. The whole situation was confusing. We decided to have her re-examined.

Because we were from the Kansas City area, we knew that the Kansas University Medical Center was just across the state line, not far from our hometowns of Independence and Buckner. A pediatrician recommended an audiologist there who had special equipment for testing children, so we made an appointment. The first mutually agreeable time available was in July, two months away. When the time arrived, Rainelle accompanied Jennifer on the 150-mile trip. I had to stay in Columbia to go to classes. When Rainelle came home she was ecstatic.

"Jennifer's not deaf!" she said, barely able to contain herself. "They said she's got a mild hearing loss. I watched them test her, and she did respond to the sound!"

I was puzzled.

"What did they say was her problem then?" I asked.

"They're not sure, and they want to do more tests," Rainelle said. "They think she just tunes out sound she doesn't want to hear."

We looked at each other, happy and hopeful. Maybe Jennifer's problem could be fixed. We hugged each other and then, with Jennifer, went to McDonald's to eat and celebrate.

On hearing the new diagnosis, all the grandparents were very happy. They knew it all along, they said.

"I didn't think that baby was deaf," my mother said. "She just looked like she understood what we said to her."

"She's just outsmarting us," Rainelle's mother said, and we all agreed that Jennifer was probably a very smart little girl who would have to be taught not to tune us out.

"I remember George used to act like he couldn't hear sometimes, like when I told him to clean up his room," my mother added. We all agreed that Jennifer might be as contrary as I had been.

Audiology Report, 7/21/71
Jennifer Harris, age 19 months

The child was placed in a sound field and stimulated with narrow bands of calibrated noise, white noise, and monitored live voice. Localizing responses, with considerable response latency and rapid response adaptation, were noted to narrow bands of noises with center frequencies ranging between 5C and 6kHz at presentation levels ranging between 20 and 40 dB. We were able to obtain response to monitored live voice consistently at 30 dB although we were unable to elicit any specific reflexive responses from the child. Again, this child was able to localize sound in sound field, and her adaptation to testing procedures is notable at this time. In summary, our initial impression of this child is that she could have no more than a mild hearing impairment. Observation given to us by the parents of the child's response to sound in the home, as well as the history, tend to confirm our test results.

We were careful to point out to the parents that our conclusions are tentative at best, and that further extensive audiological evaluation will be required. We definitely contraindicated the use of any type of hearing aid at the present time, until a more definitive assessment of the child's auditory abilities can be completed.

Summary:

Observation and behavioral test results indicate no more than a mild peripheral hearing impairment. However, our diagnosis must be considered only tentative at this time, and further audiological, psychological and otological evaluation will be necessary. Systematic parental observation, scheduling with psychology, otology and audiology in early September, and electro-physiological assessment of auditory sensitivity were strongly recommended. Additional recommendations will be contingent upon further assessment in early September.

September 1971 arrived, bringing the start of another school year. I still associate the smell of new denim with September, because that's when my parents always took me shopping for new school clothes. Autumn is the smell of new blue jeans followed by the smells of fallen leaves and apple cider. It's my favorite time of year. But that autumn— like the preceding seasons—was beginning to be connected with the smell of dirty diapers, which were everywhere. Jennifer, now 21 months old, went through lots of diapers. She was so skinny that it was difficult to make them fit snugly. Her entire outfit had to be changed frequently because her diapers didn't catch all that they should.

But Jennifer was still cute. She had tiny features and very little baby fat. She seemed to be growing tall without adding to her fourteen pounds. She was able to stand by herself. That's when we noticed that her flat feet splayed out, the opposite of being pigeon-toed. What a sight. Her doctors recommended orthopedic shoes to help her walk.

Rainelle and I often talked about Jennifer, but the conversations didn't seem to lead anywhere. If she wasn't deaf, why didn't she talk? Why was she gaining weight so slowly? Was she going to have to wear ugly shoes the rest of her life? Well, we didn't know.

We didn't even know what had caused all of this. Some of the doctors said rubella, but Rainelle wasn't aware that she'd had measles during her pregnancy. We avoided openly wondering about each other's genetic make-up. One must be careful not to touch a flame.

Jennifer was also becoming less and less pleasant to be around. She seemed to cry constantly and sleep rarely. Nothing seemed to appease her. If we picked her up, she might stop crying for a moment and then resume, as though in an infant rage, her face red with anger.

"Rainelle, just let her cry," I said impatiently. "She won't stop if you pick her up."

"But I can't stand to hear her cry," Rainelle snapped as we glared at each other. She picked Jennifer up and began to rock her.

Time came for Jennifer's "return" to her audiologists. We anxiously anticipated the visit to see if they could explain what was happening. I was taking psychology courses at the university which left me impressed with the merits of science and its ability to answer questions. I hoped the highly trained professionals could come up with explanations and solutions for Jennifer's problems. I hoped and I expected.

The audiologist recommended a visit with a child psychologist in addition to the audiological testing. So Rainelle took Jennifer for the appointment. When they returned, Rainelle was livid.

"All those fancy degrees and no help," she said.

"What happened?" I asked.

"Well, this woman takes Jennifer for fifteen minutes, plays with her, and then acts like she understands her. But she can't tell me what's wrong with Jennifer or what to do next. Why did I go there anyway? For her to tell me less than I already knew?"

I defended the psychologist.

"They see lots of children," I said. "She was just trying to be cautious."

"Oh, so I'm the unreasonable mother, am I? You all have me analyzed and I'm crazy, is that it?"

I couldn't find words to respond calmly to this outburst. I told Rainelle that we should discuss this again when we were more reasonable. I might as well have told her to go to her room until she could act nicer.

Several years later I obtained a copy of the psychologist's report.

Name: Harris, Jennifer
Birth Date: 12/2/69
Date of Report: 9/71

Referral:
This child was being treated as a possible post-rubella hearing impaired child for a number of months and was referred to Dr. Johanson for audiometric assessment. This summer he saw her and felt that the child did not have a hearing impairment on a peripheral basis. He raised some question about her behavioral repertoire in areas other than the auditory and referred her for our opinion. The family is returning to Columbia, Missouri, so the father can complete his B.A. degree, but we hope to complete the evaluation here at the Medical Center.

Observation of the Child:
This is a scrawny, monkey-like girl who certainly has many of the physical signs of post-rubella syndrome. She was quite easy to work with in play situations and she interacted well with Miss Dixon and myself, not clinging to the mother in any sense. She is more like a 12 to 14 month-old child in terms of the repertoire of behaviors that she demonstrated, but with us she gave evidence of perseverance, good attention, and all other behaviors that are necessary for learning how to manipulate learning materials. She related readily to us; she followed some of our grosser gestural instruction and she herself did some gesturing of a communicative nature. She smiled readily and returned for praise and smiles to the people who were administering them. Thus, in terms of one of Dr. Johanson's questions, we do not see her as a child who is turned off from social interactions.

The child did not really ever respond to sound during the evaluation. We had timers, buzzers, and telephones going, but at one point the mother did seem able to get the child's attention by calling her. Several times Jennifer threw toys on the floor and once when I yelled "no" at her she may have modified her behavior. . . .

Essentially, I see this as a child who is not responding to the world of sound, who is fairly attentive and responsive to adults, and who is developing a very crude gestural system. The fact that she has a gross communication system is no guarantee that she will elaborate on this, as we are finding with some of the older post-rubella children. I plan to see the mother when she returns to see Dr. Johanson in two weeks and at that time will be able to work out some kind of program for the child in her community. In the interim week I gave the mother some suggestions for reading.

A copy of the psychologist's report was forwarded to the audiologist but not to us. (Even to this day, we don't get copies of professional reports unless we ask for them, and then they are released reluctantly.) Shortly thereafter we went to the appointment with the audiologist hoping for some resolution of Jennifer's problems, or at least some direction about where to go and what to do now.

I attended this testing session. Dr. Johanson, the audiologist, introduced himself. He appeared to be in his early thirties, confident and forceful as he shook my hand. He smiled warmly as he picked up Jennifer and hugged her. No painted smile here, I thought, and I relaxed.

Dr. Johanson explained the testing procedure. Inside a soundproof chamber were three or four speakers. He could direct his voice to any of the speakers from a control booth separated from the chamber by a one-way mirror. On top of each speaker sat a toy animal, such as a duck.

The tester could manipulate the animals from the control booth. The procedure was to speak to Jennifer, who was sitting inside the soundproof chamber, and randomly to switch speakers. If Jennifer oriented to a speaker, indicating she could locate the direction of the sound, then the tester rewarded her by making the animals light up and wings flap. The assumption was that children enjoy watching the animals perform and would quickly associate the act of turning toward the sound with the pleasure of seeing the animals.

Rainelle and I stood in the control booth with Dr. Johanson. Jennifer could not see us. We watched as he began.

"Jennifer, look here," he commanded after flipping a switch. Jennifer sat motionless.

"Jennifer, here," he said again, and Jennifer looked toward the duck, which lit up and flapped its wings.

Jennifer, startled, began to cry.

"That's okay," Dr. Johanson said. "Watch." He paused for ten seconds.

"Jennifer, look here," he said. Jennifer turned abruptly toward another speaker, and its rabbit hopped. The testing continued. As the ducks flapped and the rabbits hopped, Jennifer cried. But she looked at them. By God, she looked at them!

I couldn't figure out what the trick was.

"Why does she hear in that chamber and nowhere else?" I asked Dr. Johanson. "What does this mean?"

"Jennifer just doesn't respond to sound in her environment," he said. "Her auditory channels function, but her brain doesn't attend to the impulses. We don't know why; we can only recommend that you work with some people in your home community to monitor Jennifer's progress and help her communicate in whatever way she can, using gestures if necessary." Dr. Johanson then began talking about a program at the mental health center back in Columbia. He wanted us to check it out.

We left the office with Jennifer, got into our car, and drove home still confused. We were wary of yet another program to investigate. But maybe this one would have an answer.

Audiology Report, September 1971
Jennifer Harris, age 21 months

Dr. Breckenridge from the Psychology Department sat in on the interpretation to the family (mother). The mother is still searching for a direct definition and etiology of the problem, and did express negativism which was noted by Dr. Breckenridge during her previous evaluation. We both felt that these parents are in need of immediate help, and made the following recommendations:

1. The parents and Dr. Johanson will contact Dr. Hall in Columbia to attempt to generate a treatment program.
2. Treatment should be directed at controlling behavior and developing a rudimentary gestural system for this child.
3. She should be re-evaluated in six months, when both an otological and audiological evaluation should be completed.
4. Medical records should be reviewed with Dr. Busby to determine whether any further medical treatment is warranted.

Summary:
Results of behavioral and ear measurement again indicate no more than a mild auditory impairment in the better ear, and probably normal bilateral hearing sensitivity. Recommendations for immediate action concerning this child and family have been made and will be coordinated through the Psychology and Audiology Department.

The inevitable happened. The university dismissed Rainelle from school because of her grades. There had been a warning letter of probation the semester before. But this was final. Rainelle was heartbroken.

"Don't they understand the reasons for the grades?" she cried. "Why can't they let up on me a little? What's it to them anyway?"

I was my usual diplomatic self. "You didn't attend your classes," I said. "What do you expect?"

Rainelle was certainly intelligent enough to excel in college. In high school she was a champion debater who competed nationally. She and I first met at a debate tournament. She was a topnotch extemporaneous speaker with quick wit and sharp perception. She was poised and popular. But those traits weren't enough to pull her through classes she didn't attend. Though I didn't say so to her, I hurt for her because I knew she felt she had failed. But our attention was more on Jennifer's problems than on Rainelle's.

If we didn't know what was wrong with Jennifer or why, then at least we now knew there were lots of other people who didn't know either. But maybe Dr. Hall in Columbia would have some answers.

Dr. Hall was the director of the Pee Wee program to which we were referred. It was federally funded to help very young children with unusual handicaps and learning disorders. We arranged an appointment to see what the program could do.

Dr. Hall, a heavyset man with dark hair, had received the referral information from Dr. Johanson. He began the interview by reviewing the file.

"This must be puzzling to you," he said. "Jennifer hears but doesn't act like she does."

We agreed that this puzzled us.

"And nobody seems sure that rubella caused this," he continued. "So you're looking for someone to help Jennifer develop mentally any way she can. I think I should tell you that we may not be able to answer those questions either, but we can observe Jennifer over a longer period of time than anyone else has and that may give us some ideas about what to try."

He waited patiently for us to respond.

"It's getting pretty frustrating, all this uncertainty," I said, looking at Rainelle.

"I know it must be," Dr. Hall replied. "Why don't you tell me a little more about what you think about this."

I didn't know what to say exactly, and I mumbled, "Well, it gets tiring having to explain to everyone that we don't know what's wrong. Then someone will say 'look on the bright side—she could have been born deaf *and* blind.' Do you think you can help Jennifer?"

"We'll sure try," he said. "What do your families have to say about this?"

Rainelle and I looked at each other.

"They're not much help," Rainelle said. "They don't seem convinced that there's anything seriously wrong, and they don't understand what it's like living with Jennifer. She's getting hard to manage, she's not toilet-trained, she doesn't eat right. They just say all babies are like that some-times and drop the subject, like I didn't have a brain in my head. My mother tries to sympathize. But they all live so far away anyway."

We sat in silence until Dr. Hall asked if we wanted to tour the ward where the Pee Wee program operated.

"Some of the children live here all the time," he said. "I don't think Jennifer should. Since you live so close, we'd rather you bring her in for a couple of hours each afternoon."

The ward looked more like a living room than a hospital, except all the entrances and exits were locked. A throw rug lay in front of a comfortable, plain divan. There was a television, but the children ignored it. They were playing with adults.

Some of the adults were introduced as students, the others as staff. One plump, middle-aged Black woman strolled over to Jennifer.

"Who's this little girl now?" she said. "Jennifer, huh? Well, hello Jennifer. Are you gonna stay with us?" By this time Jennifer was in her arms and they were halfway across the room.

Dr. Hall laughed and asked if it was all right to leave Jennifer while we finished the tour.

As we walked along, a child lying on a cart whizzed by.

"Those are for kids who can't quite walk," Dr. Hall explained. "They can lie down on those and scoot around. They're easy to steer. Jennifer might like them. I understand she's not quite walking yet, is that right?"

We nodded and said she probably would have fun with the carts.

A lean and glossy Irish setter walked out of one of the sleeping rooms which opened into the main room, and the children gathered around. I wondered what the dog was doing in the hospital.

"That's the children's favorite therapist," Dr. Hall said. "He's their pet and friend."

We stood for a moment and watched the children pat and cuddle the dog, which then bounded away to spread cheer to another group of children.

A young woman, perhaps thirty, approached us. Her appearance was very neat. She wore a simple pullover dress, hose, and flat heels.

"I'd like you to meet Nancy," said Dr. Hall. "She'll be Jennifer's teacher. . . . Nancy, would you like to show Mr. and Mrs. Harris around a little more and talk with them about your plans for Jennifer?"

Nancy was soft-spoken and easy to talk to. She explained that she would work with Jennifer to help her gain confidence. She didn't think this would take too long, considering how readily Jennifer had gone to the housemother.

"We'll work on things like this small puzzle, and we'll just try to see what she can do," Nancy said.

So Jennifer began the Pee Wee program. Every afternoon Rainelle, who now had her driver's license, took Jennifer to the hospital, dropped her off, and then waited; there wasn't enough time for Rainelle to go anywhere before it would be time to pick Jennifer up. I sometimes took Jennifer but, because of my job, it was difficult for me to get away. I had gotten more part-time work in the biology department at school and had to be there regular hours.

While Jennifer was in the Pee Wee program, she practiced putting different shaped objects in matching holes and learned to solve simple jigsaw puzzles and to match colors and textures. Her sense of color was especially acute; she excelled at discriminating slight differences of shade. Nancy became very fond of Jennifer and talked at length with us about her, showing off her new accomplishments and remarking that she learned quickly. Rainelle and Nancy developed a good relationship, and Rainelle valued Nancy's opinions.

We celebrated Jennifer's second birthday the second day of December. As Christmas approached, she finally gained enough strength to walk. Her legs were so spindly that her balance was poor. When learning to walk, most babies fall by sitting on their diapers. Jennifer careened unpredictably, and we watched nervously to be sure she didn't fall on her face. When she did fall, we tried not to overreact. Soon she recovered from her tumbles like a grade school tomboy.

We watched her with hope, thinking that perhaps soon she would begin to listen to sounds. If she was walking, could talking be far behind?

Nancy was as confused and concerned about Jennifer's inconsistent hearing as we were.

"Sometimes Jennifer acts like she hears, and then sometimes she doesn't," Nancy said.

Jennifer and Nancy had been working together for several months when time came for another audiology examination. Nancy went to this appointment in Kansas City to watch the duck flap its wings like a Groucho Marx gag. But none of us were about to bet our lives on the outcome of the test.

When Nancy, Rainelle, and Jennifer returned, Nancy was shaking her head in disbelief. She had seen it now. Jennifer did turn toward the talking duck. But Nancy was more perplexed than before because she didn't know what the tests meant she should do for Jennifer. It was all a muddle!

Audiology Report, March 1972
Jennifer Harris, age 2 years, 3 months

Approximately half way through the evaluation Nancy entered the testing session. We placed Jennifer back in the test room and re-evaluated auditory sensitivity, so that Nancy could observe the child's responses to sound. Following the audiological evaluation, we spent considerable time with the teacher and the parent, interpreting the child's responses to sound, as well as what they might expect of the child in the future. Again, we were very impressed with the improvement in this child's overall responsiveness to socialization and to auditory stimuli.

Summary:
This child's hearing sensitivity is within normal limits. Recommendations for further testing of hearing and psychological development were made above.

Except for my first year of college, when I was not married, I didn't participate very much in the usual extracurricular college activities. Nevertheless, Jennifer was not the sole focus of Rainelle's life nor of my own.

Rainelle was interested in political science and literature. She read voraciously, especially about the assasination of President Kennedy. Her fascination with this murder, I think, reflected her outrage that the forces of darkness could upend our lives so. Rainelle and I were both born on July 4, 1950. We were thirteen when Kennedy was killed and the visions of Camelot were taken from our teenage minds.

I became interested in animal behavior and began to take courses in psychobiology and ethology, fancy labels for the study of such things as animal aggression and territoriality. In one class, I devised an experiment to measure the pecking order of stickleback fish, sort of like figuring out who's king and queen of the aquarium.

In another class I wanted to investigate whether box turtles had ritual displays of aggression. My first task was to find some turtles. So Rainelle and I got a babysitter for Jennifer, and we went turtle hunting. We tromped through the woods, kicking leaves aside in hopes of finding turtles for my mad scientist adventure. On crisp, clear afternoons we thrashed our way through the underbrush, glad that our prey couldn't run fast when it heard noise. We were excited when we uncovered a turtle, and we laughed as we played peek-a-boo games with the shy creatures inside the shells.

For some reason, turtles like to travel on the wet country roads. So a good time to go on a "turtle run" was after a night rain. At the slightest hint of rain, we would yell,

"Turtle run, turtle run!" and scamper to the car. Rainelle would bundle up Jennifer in pajamas that could be cinched at the bottom to keep feet from sticking out. In these pajamas Jennifer looked like Popeye's Swee'pea. While Jennifer slept in the back seat of the car, Rainelle and I would try to catch sight of the creatures in the beam of the car's headlights.

Turtle runs alternated with doughnut runs—midnight expeditions to the all-night doughnut store. We knew just when the fresh doughnuts came out of the oven; so did half the denizens of the college dormitories, and we often stood in line to get the warm glazed rolls. Sometimes we stopped first at the all-night grocery store for a carton of milk to wash down the treat. I remember Rainelle, tall and pretty, drinking her milk and eating her doughnuts. Like all the other coeds there, she wore clothing hastily donned for the late night excursion.

But my college days were coming to an end. It was the last semester of my senior year in college, a period of reassessment and redirection. I had thought about trying graduate school at the University of Missouri in Columbia, but Rainelle protested, saying she wanted to move back to Kansas City, apparently so she could be closer to her mother. I understood, and we both figured that there would be good schools for Jennifer in Kansas City. She was three years old and no longer really an infant. The Pee Wee program had been good, the people nice, but there had to be other places like it.

I had chosen a psychology major in college because it left me time to take courses in computer programming, a practical vocation. I enjoyed psychology but knew it wasn't a very saleable degree in the job market. On a whim, I applied for graduate school in psychology at the University of Missouri in Kansas City and was accepted. I had spent much time looking, unsuccessfully, for work as a programmer. The university offered me financial aid which included a part-time job as a computer operator. I accepted it, thinking this would be the experience I needed to move into better programming jobs. So after I graduated from college in May 1972, we moved to Kansas City.

Prior to the move, Rainelle also applied for admission to the university branch in Kansas City and was admitted on probation. We were both thrilled. Here was another chance for her to complete her undergraduate study. We found an apartment, Rainelle began summer school, and I started working in the computer center while waiting for classes to begin in the fall.

We were still concerned about Jennifer's problems. The Kansas University Medical Center was nearby, and we found that Jennifer could participate in its special programs. With my mornings free, I could take Jennifer to her speech therapy sessions Monday through Thursday and her occupational therapy session Friday. It seemed that everyone in the family was making progress in school.

Jennifer was not making much progress at home, however. She was increasingly restless and destructive. Not only was she not toilet-trained but she was now very mobile. When she had a bowel movement, she frequently removed her diapers and smeared the walls, fingerpainting with her excrement. At night, I slept fitfully, expecting at any moment to hear Jennifer out of bed making ugly, smelly, brown designs on the wall. We didn't know how to stop her. We felt angry and helpless. Rainelle was as frustrated as I and ventilated feelings by yelling, which apparently was harmless to Jennifer.

Jennifer's cardiac and orthopedic care was transferred to the Kansas City Children's Hospital. A special program funded by the state paid most of the financial but none of the psychic costs of going to the hospital.

Like most institutions, the hospital had its faults. The initial panic set in when looking for a parking space. There were lots of empty spaces with "Doctors Only" signs. I wished I'd paid more attention in the course on class, status, and power. After twenty minutes of circling, looking for a space, I usually became convinced that the Hospital Authority towed cars without engines to the parking lot so the place would look full.

That notion was demolished once I got into the hospital and saw the long lines in the waiting room. By this time I was already feeling irritated because the walk from car to hospital was spiced with dropped books, cookies, diapers, and toys which I had brought in anticipation of spending the better part of a day in a hospital waiting room with a highly mobile, very active, and easily bored child.

I usually managed to get in the wrong line. After fifteen minutes of waiting, I was told to go to the "other" line, which was nonexistent when I first came in but now queued back past the water fountain.

If I made it to the front of the check-in line, I often found I'd forgotten my plastic ID card. Naturally, I couldn't proceed further until a new one was made, requiring that I stand in another line. Then I had to return to the check-in line, which now extended past the water fountain and was stretching for the elevators. It all felt so impersonal. Jennifer and I were treated as little more than numbers on a plastic card.

The faces of the other adults in the clinic line looked lifeless—visages drained of expression. They all appeared poor and all seemed to be used to waiting. The bureaucracy has an equalizing effect; everyone is treated impersonally.

The doctors and other staff seemed insulated from the indignities. A few of them acted annoyed when someone asked for simple directions or information. They didn't appear to understand the frustration of waiting and standing in line and fighting red tape and waiting some more. But then, as one Russian writer said about the guards in Stalin's internment camps during the Soviet winter, how can one man who's warm understand a man who's cold?

Surely, I wondered, some of these doctors and administrators themselves must have been patients in a public clinic at one time. They of all people should want to change the dehumanizing conditions. But perhaps those who have been cold and now are warm have the shortest memories. Or maybe the sheer numbers of people make it impossible for services to be delivered efficiently let alone humanely.

The wait might have been tolerable except for the squirming, twisting, crying, kicking child attached to my right hand. Other parents at least had the release of being able to yell at their children, but I usually felt foolish doing that when Jennifer acted like she couldn't hear me anyway. Moreover, if Jennifer did manage to get away from me, there was no sense yelling—I just had to run after her.

After our preliminary visits to the hospital for routine procedures, a lengthy heart examination was scheduled for Jennifer. We went through all the lines, completed all our paperwork, sat through all the tests, and then waited in a small, bare office for the doctor's interpretation.

The cardiologist was from India. He spoke English adequately, but I had to strain to understand through the confusing accent.

"Your daughter's heart is doing fine," he said.

"So there are no problems?" we asked.

"Not for now. Sometimes she may need to have some additional work, but it is no problem now. Just if she goes to a dentist or gets infection, you should tell the doctor about her heart, and we will help him medicate her properly—just precaution, you know. She has a risk of developing extra problems with her heart if not medicated."

"Okay," I said. "Oh, we also wanted to ask about what effects her heart might have on her behavior. Is there any medication that might help her sleep better and not cry so much?"

"No, no, her behavior is normal for a retarded child. Of course we don't know how much she will be able to learn to outgrow these things, and. . ."

He continued talking, but I could only stare at him. He had said *retarded*. Who was this jerk heart doctor to call Jennifer retarded?

". . . and time will tell if she will be educable or will have to be put into an institution," he finished.

Silently, Rainelle and I got up to leave. Rainelle looked pale. I wanted to strangle the heart doctor. Rainelle was more polite. She wanted him deported.

It wasn't that retardation had never occurred to us but that it just didn't make sense. Jennifer didn't look retarded. In fact, she was very cute. She didn't drool or act dull. Her eyes were bright and attentive. She was active; she solved puzzles and showed curiosity about things around her. But then, why hadn't she walked until she was two and why wasn't she talking now? Maybe the problem with her brain was more serious than we thought.

At dinner the clink of forks on our plates was deafening.

CHAPTER 3

The summer passed quickly. Rainelle was doing well in her classes. Jennifer was being taught simple sign language. She responded quickly, learning signs for *yes, sit down, good girl,* and *all gone.* Given this progress, we pushed aside thoughts of retardation and hoped for some kind of breakthrough with Jennifer's hearing problem.

The speech therapist and her supervisor, an audiologist who was a colleague of the man who had been testing Jennifer, seemed impatient with me when we talked about Jennifer. But I couldn't pinpoint why. I did notice that they both referred to Jennifer as deaf, a diagnosis which didn't make sense to me; the other audiologist's reports claimed that she had normal hearing.

Nevertheless, as the summer drew to an end, Rainelle and I began discussing the preschool program for the deaf conducted at the Children's Hospital where Jennifer's postsurgery follow-up was done. The therapist and supervisor recommended we enroll Jennifer. I promised that we would investigate the program even though I wasn't convinced. It seemed reasonable to take a look at what was available, but I did not guarantee to enroll Jennifer. I had thumbed through the Yellow Pages and had found another preschool program that seemed to be equipped to deal with Jennifer's behavior problems but not with her speech. The therapist frowned when I mentioned this option, saying she didn't know much about it. Her attitude left little room for discussion. This was our last meeting with Jennifer's summer helpers. I went home feeling intimidated to do things their way or else.

Progress Report
Speech and Occupational Therapy, August 1972

Jennifer is very small for her age (weight 20 lbs. at 2½ years of age) and appears fragile. Rubella titers are to be done to determine whether or not Jennifer is a post-rubella child. Muscle strength, at least in the upper extremities, is decreased. She could not push pop beads together, and informal testing revealed she either could not maintain a position against resistance or did not understand that she was to do this. More complete muscle testing and reflex testing will be done at a later date. Jennifer does display good protective and optical righting reflexes. Gross motor skills are comparable to those of a 12–18 month old child. Jennifer does not jump in place, balance momentarily on one foot, kick a ball forward, or walk backwards as is expected of a 2½ year old child. Fine motor skills are at the 16–20 month developmental level. Jennifer uses her index finger for pointing; a neat pincer prehension of thumb to index finger was exhibited. This is noted repeatedly as she picked up blocks, raisins, etc. Jennifer stacked 5 blocks, alternating the use of both hands and crossing the body midline with each hand. She did not copy or imitate the drawing of a vertical or horizontal line or circle but perseverated in scribbling. She used a full palmar grasp with the pencil. She did spontaneously dump a raisin from a bottle. . . .

In summary, we would make the following recommendations regarding Jennifer's speech development:
1. That the family continue in the program at Children's Hospital.
2. Our impression is that the question of whether or not Jennifer has a hearing loss at this point is somewhat academic. Jennifer shows no indication (during the 23 sessions this semester) that she used her hearing for any purpose. Therefore, some kind of procedure for teaching children who do not use hearing is in order.

3. If the parents request to return to this program, we are not interested in working with the child unless the parents are willing *to become involved in some type of counseling situation which helps the two of them view their child more realistically* (emphasis mine).

My first encounter with the personnel of the Children's Hospital preschool for the deaf was irritating. The director of children's services couldn't answer my questions about fees; the business office didn't know what services were to be offered, so a fee couldn't be determined. Nonetheless, believing that the money would just have to be found somewhere, Rainelle and I filled out all the necessary forms and arranged for all referral information to be forwarded. The director set a date for us to be interviewed by the full social service staff.

Rainelle, Jennifer, and I went to the hospital on the appointed day. We were met by the director, who took us to the interview room. As we entered, we observed a semicircular table around which sat six people, several of whom were dressed in white laboratory coats. I felt as though my nose should twitch and sniff for the tunnel that led to the cheese. The director motioned us toward chairs squarely facing the people sitting behind the table. All of them were reading papers pulled from folders opened in front of them.

A psychiatrist began the questioning. I knew she was a psychiatrist because she had an accent Sigmund Freud would have loved.

"Vell, vy do yo vant to bring your child to thees program?" she asked.

Shrewd opening, but I parried, "Because we think she may be deaf."

This banter continued for about fifteen minutes. They finally huddled and agreed to let Jennifer enroll. I was not sure if the interview was a mere formality or just a chance to gawk at the parents. Incidentally, the committee wasn't sure about the fees for the program either. We then met

Jennifer's teacher, who seemed interested and competent. We got a schedule of classes which would start in early September. Everything seemed set.

Feeling apprehensive but hopeful, I dropped Jennifer off for her first day of school. Jennifer went to the teacher without fussing. I left quickly, thinking she was in good hands. My first graduate classes started that same day. I went to school relieved of responsibility for Jennifer for a while. It was nice.

At the end of the school day, I went to pick up Jennifer. Eager to see how her day had gone, I walked into her classroom. Jennifer was curled up on the floor sobbing uncontrollably. I had never seen her cry this way. She seemed scared, a behavior very uncharacteristic of Jennifer, who usually appeared angry when she cried.

When Jennifer saw me, she rushed into my arms, also an uncharacteristic act. She buried her face against my chest and continued to sob. Wearing a headband that had two pipe cleaners sticking out like feathers from her forehead, she looked like a skinny bumblebee. She was such a pathetic little girl.

I turned to the teacher. "What happened?"

"Oh, we put the headphones on her, and it scared her, I guess."

"Is that usual, to put headphones on children their first day in class?"

"Well, I talked with the psychiatrist, and she said it was okay."

"What the hell does she know about it!" I was furious. Why is a psychiatrist an expert on everything? I didn't say what I was thinking, that this kind of incompetence was intolerable. I did say that Jennifer probably wouldn't return the next day. Then I turned and left with Jennifer clutching me.

We sat in the car and rocked until she was calm. I wondered what to do next.

Rainelle and I agreed not to have Jennifer continue in the deaf preschool, so we went to our second choice, the Foundation School for Retarded Children. Although we didn't think Jennifer exactly fit the retarded label, her lack of speech, high activity level, toilet habits, and general fussiness meant that some type of special school was necessary. Besides, we simply didn't know where else to turn.

The director of the Foundation School had a retarded son who was in a perpetual care institution.

"My boy doesn't look retarded either," he said at our first meeting, pausing for a moment to stare out the window. Then, more to himself than to us, he continued quietly.

"Beautiful physique. He's seventeen now, but his mind never was right. Such a shame. My wife just couldn't accept it. We see the boy every month, but he'll never be out of the institution."

He turned to address us directly, his voice strong.

"Some kids here can learn to be independent though. We have sheltered workshops where they learn work skills. Simple things, sure, but useful. We'll just have to see how Jennifer fits in and what she can do."

The classrooms at the school were small but adequate. We met the woman who would be Jennifer's teacher. She seemed nice. The tuition was only a little more than regular daycare. Everyone seemed to like Jennifer, so we agreed to send her.

Several weeks passed. Jennifer was adapting to her environment, but she wasn't learning and improving. Her classmates, Down's syndrome children and one little girl who had been oxygen-deprived at birth, became models for Jennifer. Rainelle became angry when Jennifer began to stand with her mouth half open, her tongue lolling.

"That's disgusting," Rainelle said. "Jennifer never did that before she went there. How is Jennifer going to get better when she's around retarded kids all day? She's going to act just like them. We have to do something."

"I agree," I said, "but where is there something better? No regular preschool will take her because she's too much trouble. There just isn't anything else, so don't yell at me unless you've got an idea."

Rainelle was always more polite to strangers than I. She seldom directly expressed her anger or frustration about Jennifer's schools. Instead, she told me, and I assumed she expected me to act on it—an expectation that I resented.

Jennifer's behavior at home became progressively worse. We were all tense and irritable. My job at the computer center ended when summer was over. I took a job waiting tables at Stephenson's Apple Farm Restaurant and continued in graduate school, and Rainelle continued her classes. There wasn't time to do more than clean dirty diapers, go to class, and serve barbecued chicken to demanding ingrates.

We survived the school year but knew something had to change.

[Diary, March 1973]

When she finally went to sleep tonight, I was relieved and at the same time ashamed. The evening began with her refusal to eat supper. I had insisted that she eat despite her lack of interest. Later, she badgered me incessantly for something to drink, and I was angry at her stubbornness.

In her normal, unending movement, which sets my very soul on edge, she continued the evening. From couch to tattered chair, to light switch and beyond, my little girl raced. She ripped a book, took off her shoes, and turned off the television show, which was in its final act when the villain meets his well-deserved finish. I turned the set back on, and she proceeded to turn up the volume to a mind-scrambling roar. She whined and whimpered, demanding another drink.

As I told her no for the hundredth time that evening, I smelled her dirty pants—and I was furious. She refuses to be toilet-trained. I say refuse when perhaps I shouldn't. Jennifer doesn't know what I want from her. Why don't I tell her? Because she can't talk. Why can't she talk? Because she can't hear, and she doesn't hear not because she can't but because she won't (at least that's the current professional opinion). She probably doesn't hear for the same reason that she runs frantically around the house tearing the cushions off the chairs and the pictures off the walls—some sort of brain damage.

I find the real experts' explanations (how many have there been) as worthless as my own, and just as confusing. Let's face it, nobody knows what's wrong with her, not many care, and it probably doesn't matter anyway; what can they do.

I spanked her until my hand was red and smelled like her bottom. She looked so hurt, not physically, but in her eyes. She buried her head in my chest, covering her eyes. She made me ashamed I'd lost my temper, so ashamed.

Jennifer is long but skinny, and as she climbed back into my lap, still whimpering, she stuck her bony elbows squarely into my ribs. I didn't care because she sits in my lap so rarely. Normally squirming, jumping, and running, she seldom allows me to feel the pleasure of her warmth or the smell of her moist baby breath for more than two seconds. The frustration is like having intimacy interrupted by your partner's drawing away for lack of interest, leaving an empty longing and feeling of inadequacy.

She stayed in my arms rubbing my whiskers, now twelve hours old, with her fingertips. Her arms went limp, her eyelids closed, and all thirty underweight pounds of her sagged. I saw her furry golden hair, knotted and twisted by nervous fingers. I held her close.

Everyone from grandparents to friends knows what's wrong with my skinny little kid, and they all have thousands of well-intentioned suggestions. But they don't live with her every day. As I looked at her in my arms, my heart cried for her and for us, and my stomach knotted. Living with her is hard, but I decided to keep her one more day to try again.

It was frustrating to be so dependent upon speech therapists, physicians, and psychologists, none of whom had been much help so far. Still believing that Jennifer's speech problems might be treatable, I decided to do something myself. I enrolled in a graduate course with the ominous title, "Experimental Analysis of Clinical Behavior." I learned behavior modification techniques with the intention of working with Jennifer myself.

In addition to classroom instruction, the course required a practicum. I got myself assigned to a professor at the Kansas University Medical Center's child rehabilitation unit. He worked with speech-delayed children, children who don't talk for several years despite normal hearing. For several weeks I observed the procedures being used on one child, Edie.

Edie's grandmother brought her to school every day. An advanced graduate student took Edie to a vacant room and began the session by placing her in a chair and strapping her in. Then the wait began. At first, Edie screamed in protest, wanting her grandmother, wanting free. She was ignored. After two or three sessions of an hour each, she finally quieted down.

Edie remained silent for one more session. The teacher stayed in the room with her but said and did nothing. Suddenly Edie looked up and softly murmured "mmmm." The teacher quickly looked at her, smiled, enthusiastically said "good girl, Edie!" and gave her an M&M candy. Edie devoured her treat.

Within a few weeks Edie was saying simple words. She was rewarded only for progressively more complex utterances; eventually she was rewarded only for complete sentences.

This was exciting to watch. I was eager to begin with Jennifer.

My chance came soon. I brought Jennifer to the hospital for our sessions. She sat whining in her chair the first several days. During one session she soiled her diapers. It was against procedure to allow anything to interfere with the work, because that would teach Jennifer that there were ways other than full cooperation to end the session. So we sat in the cramped, unventilated room that now reeked of excrement.

After a few more days, Jennifer tried smiling to win my sympathies. "Daddy, daddy," I could imagine her saying, "this is hard. Let me out. Oh please let me out."

But I was tough. I wouldn't give in. On the twelfth day Jennifer uttered "mmma."

I was so surprised I almost forgot to reward her with the M&M.

Jennifer looked at the M&M and threw it on the floor.

I picked it up and gave it back to her, thinking she had not recognized what it was.

She threw it again.

The next session I came prepared with a bottle of Coke and an eyedropper. When Jennifer saw the bottle, her eyes danced. She held out her arms, pleading for a drink. I refused and assumed my role of ignoring her. Midway through the hour Jennifer said "mmma." Quickly I squirted an eyedropper full of Coke into her mouth.

Jennifer was pleased, and within a few days she began to make sounds more frequently.

The objective was to reward Jennifer for making common vowel and consonant sounds and for matching these sounds with pictures of objects. For example, "O" would be paired with an orange; Jennifer would be rewarded if she said "O" when shown an orange. I trained her to say "mmma," "oh," "ahhh," and several other sounds.

I had great hopes that Jennifer would soon talk like Edie. Maybe all this work would stimulate the part of Jennifer's brain that wasn't functioning.

Jennifer seemed to look forward to the sessions. With her skinny little legs protruding from her diapers, she always marched over to her chair at the beginning of each session and sat down. Before I had a chance to get set up, she began.

"Oh, ahh, ahh, mmma," she said, in no apparent order and with no apparent connection to anything.

Try as I might, I could not get her to connect sounds with pictures. Fortunately for both of us, the practicum soon ended.

We began the frustrating search for a new school for Jennifer. In one of my classes with a faculty member who used behavior modification techniques, I learned of another preschool—Operation Discovery—that took kids with special problems and used graduate students as teachers. It was another alley to explore, at least.

We had to find something that worked with Jennifer, not just to aid her language development but to control her behavior at home, which was getting progressively worse. Jennifer was getting very good at opening doors and containers, but she had not learned what was dangerous and what was safe.

Whether or not Jennifer was ever hyperactive is doubtful, but she definitely was active and difficult to control. The gap between her adventuring spirit and sound judgment was particularly large and dangerous.

Even if there had been no risk in allowing Jennifer to explore freely, it was difficult for Rainelle and me to get needed rest and relaxation if Jennifer was holding the flour container and preparing to dump its contents on the kitchen floor. Because she was deaf, yelling at her from a distance got absolutely no results. Once in a while a foot stomp on the floor would create enough vibration to get her attention. It was usually necessary to get up, walk to Jennifer wherever she was getting into trouble, and take care of the problem. Many times Jennifer only sounded like she was getting into mischief, but a false alarm had to be investigated just the same. Considerable time and effort was spent trying to protect Jennifer from the house and the house from Jennifer.

Almost from the time she became mobile, we needed to find ways to corral her so we could save our sanity and get some rest. The first constraint was, of course, a playpen. While Jennifer was quite young, this worked well. But she quickly outgrew it and became frustrated by such confinement.

We attached latches to exits to prevent Jennifer from opening doors and going outside. There was absolutely no way to communicate to her that we didn't want her to go out; of course, we couldn't explain the reasons either. Physical restraint was the only alternative. Even when she was allowed to roam, certain rooms of the house had to be closed and locked. It was impossible to explain to her that she should stay out of drawers and away from makeup and bottles of dangerous substances.

Since birth Jennifer threw "fits of rage" (for lack of a better description) in which she would thrash about and cry angrily, though she never seemed to cry real tears. I don't think it's fair to call these tantrums, because she didn't seem to be reacting to disappointment or to circumstances. Her fits just seemed to arise without cause, much like a bad mood that most people inexplicably suffer from time to time.

Jennifer's moods probably resulted from both an inability to communicate and brain damage. Whatever the reason, we couldn't allow her to hurt herself by banging her head on the floor or pulling her hair. So we learned to hold her in our laps and pin her arms by encircling her in our arms. After five or ten minutes, calm would usually return, and we would have avoided punishing her for something she couldn't help doing.

We also used this hold while visiting friends because we usually didn't trust Jennifer out of our sight. The constant necessity of physically restraining her was very tiring and irritating for Rainelle and me. We couldn't just relax and visit.

I decided to build a playroom in the basement for Jennifer. It was built so she could be locked in, to prevent her from reaching the furnace and water heater. I was afraid she would tamper with these if not watched, and the main purpose of the playroom was to make supervision less demanding.

The playroom was effective except for two problems. Jennifer didn't want to be confined, so she would throw toys against the paneled wall and create a racket that was deafening to me. When that tactic got no response, she would have a bowel movement and then smear it all over everything, as if to punish me for locking her away. The "padded cell," complete with carpet and paneling, created about as much trouble as respite.

On many occasions, tired from a day's work, I tried to outwit Jennifer, thinking that she would calm down if just left alone. Instead, the intensity of her mood often increased. Sometimes as Rainelle and I sat listening to Jennifer wreaking havoc in the basement, the odor of excrement wafted up to us. Each of us waited for the other to move first, to face the onerous task of cleaning up the mess. I was tired of this constant burden.

With the spring of 1973 approaching, we visited the behavior modification school, Operation Discovery, to see what they had to offer. Although the school wasn't designed specifically for children with language problems, the staff said they might be able to help Jennifer by introducing language visually, through both written words and simple hand signs. In addition, they said that they could help Jennifer to develop social skills and improve her behavior.

We wanted to make some decision, but we felt like rabbits standing on the center line of a busy highway. No one direction seemed especially good.

Soon it was time for yet another audiological examination. In just seven months Jennifer would be four years old, and she still was not talking or even close to it. She knew a few simple signs, but my project to teach her speech had failed. We had removed her from the pre-school for the deaf and the substitute program had been a stopgap measure at best. Uncertain about what to do, we hoped the audiologist could give us some ideas.

Rainelle took Jennifer to the appointment and explained her progress through the year. The audiologist examined Jennifer but made no comment when we described what had happened to Jennifer at the preschool for the deaf. We explained that Jennifer had been at the Foundation School but that it was less than ideal for her. Then we asked him about Operation Discovery. He wasn't familiar with it but liked how it sounded. He encouraged us to try it, saying that Jennifer really needed to begin gaining some language, if not through speech then through sight or sign.

"She's not deaf as we ordinarily think of it, but she acts deaf and that's what counts," he said.

Audiology Report, May 1973
Jennifer Harris, age 3 years, 5 months

We feel it imperative that this child be placed in a pre-school setting as soon as possible. The parents have applied to and been accepted at Operation Discovery pre-school, and we reinforce their contact. The mode through which this child will need to learn communication skills is as yet unspecified. Manual and visual forms of communication have been successful with children who show a similar type of auditory dysfunction, but whether or not this child will be able to communicate remains questionable. We do feel that immediate pre-school placement is imperative.

Summary:
Results of pure tone and speech audiometric test techniques indicate normal bilateral auditory sensitivity. It is also clear that Jennifer functions as a deaf child and will need a specialized type of educational instruction in order to learn communication skills. Placement in the Operation Discovery pre-school was strongly recommended, and the child should be reevaluated audiologically in 6 months.

Jennifer's orthopedic problems weren't getting worse, but her walk was still awkward as a newborn colt's. When she tried to run, her legs were stiff; when she knelt and tried to sit on her heels, her calves flopped over to one side as though torn from the knee joint. It didn't bother her, but it made me grit my teeth in sympathetic agony. To compound her walking problem, Jennifer was taller than normal for her age but weighed at least fifteen pounds less than average.

As much as I dreaded it, I once again took Jennifer to the orthopedic clinic at the Children's Hospital in Kansas City. The experience was very frustrating. The hospital had a "magic" system whereby a patient's central file was supposed to be sent to the particular clinic where the person was being seen that day. Jennifer's file must have had feet of its own; it never arrived where it should. On this particular day the receptionist continually asked, "Are you sure you're supposed to be in the orthopedic clinic?" The implication was that whatever clinic the file arrived at was therefore the correct clinic, and wherever the file wasn't couldn't be the right one.

After an hour of this, I became ill-tempered.

"Yes, damn it, I'm in the right place," I snarled.

The receptionist probably replied with something like "let me see now," but I never heard it because by this time Jennifer was racing down the hall looking for the next county and I had to track her down.

All the orthopedic appointments for the entire day were scheduled for 8:00 a.m., as nearly as I could tell. However, I didn't notice anyone being taken before 9:00 a.m. When I asked why, the answer was "Doctors are in surgery." When I asked again, I got an honest answer, "Doctors are having coffee." Now it's fine for the doctors to have coffee, but I wished they'd scheduled their appointments after coffee time. And it's hard to imagine many emergency orthopedic surgeries that couldn't be anticipated.

Jennifer and I waited five hours, until after lunch, at which time the doctor told me Jennifer's feet looked okay to him and why didn't I schedule another appointment in six months. Feeling very old and tired, I went home with Jennifer. A good night's sleep helped to allay the self-image of a rabbit smashed by a Mack truck on the highway of life.

Fall 1973 arrived and Jennifer began school at Operation Discovery. The school was supervised by faculty from the University of Missouri at Kansas City, although the program itself had no university affiliation. The school mixed normal, even superior children, with handicapped kids in ungraded classrooms. Walls in the building were covered with behavior charts and other paraphernalia of behavioral methodology which must be seen to be believed.

The basic idea of behavior modification is that behaviors are counted over a period of time so that the effects of reinforcement or punishment can be measured. Change must be observed; subjective opinions don't count.

Jennifer's teacher was a master's level psychology major who had no teaching certificate. I wondered how the state could allow an uncertified instructor to teach in private (but approved) schools while forbidding such teachers to work in public schools. The teacher was also rather unkempt. She rarely wore shoes or washed her feet. She appeared bright, if a bit cold to the children. But her teaching seemed adequate; besides, for Jennifer this was the only show in town.

I took great pains to explain to the teacher how Rainelle and I were trying to toilet-train Jennifer, but the teacher always looked uninterested. Toilet training apparently was not one of her priorities.

Nevertheless, three months of classes passed, and Jennifer seemed to be adapting adequately. She learned to match several written words with the correct object. She didn't cry a lot either, not like she had in previous schools. One graduate student took an interest in Jennifer and worked with her daily, teaching her to identify the written names of colors.

One Friday I dropped Jennifer off at school. On my return that afternoon, I noticed a horrible odor. Jennifer was wearing the same diaper that she'd had on that morning. I drove home and immediately typed a letter.

Dear Miss Connolly,

Friday December 14 a problem occurred at the pre-school which I would like to discuss with you. I decided that a letter would emphasize my concern more so than just a conversation.

We brought Jennifer to campus early Friday because I had to be at a final exam at 9:00. We put Jennifer in disposable diapers for the period until school started at 8:45 because access to bathrooms was limited and we just wanted to keep her dry.

No one arrived at Jennifer's school room until 8:55 when I left Jennifer. We understood that you were not to be at school that day. When we picked Jennifer up from school that afternoon at 3:40 she smelled as though she had messy pants. When I got her home I discovered that indeed she was messy and apparently still wearing the same pair of disposable diapers in which she had started the day. . . .

I realize that you were not present Friday and would not have permitted this to occur. However, I expect adequate supervision of the classroom in your absence, and I am concerned that additional problems may be occurring when you are absent. If minimal custodial care is not present, I doubt that any educational progress is being made either.

I am directing this letter to you only since I trust you would not be happy with these conditions and will inform me if I have assessed the situation correctly. I hope the problem can be cleared up and guarantees made to ensure adequate substitutes for you in your absence.

Sincerely yours,
George Harris

P.S. If this letter seems a bit stiff, it's because I wrote it just after I had changed Jennifer's diapers when I got home Friday after a truly invigorating ride.

Miss Connolly dismissed the incident as a one-time occurrence. I felt as though there wasn't competence anywhere. Audiologists couldn't decide if Jennifer was deaf; orthopedic doctors couldn't get to appointments on time; preschool teachers for the deaf were scaring little children on their first day of class; and now they couldn't even change diapers.

The buzzards were circling over the carrion on the highway, waiting for the traffic to clear. There was some satisfaction knowing that they too would have to get through the dirty diapers first.

[Diary, December 1973]

From outside the apartment the sounds of playing children filtered through the window. I woke gently, surprised not to have been aroused by the screams of my own child, of necessity locked in her room. She regularly beats the sun up and wails in the early predawn hours. But if I let her out of the room, she must be watched to keep her from hurting herself while playing downstairs.

She is four years old and this is the first time she has slept an entire night. The frustration and lack of sleep have made the house a battleground . . . tense, nervous, as if under siege. I felt sure I would never get to sleep until early this morning.

I wonder why this child doesn't sleep better. I wonder why she is probably deaf and retarded, and wonder why she acts out a thousand moods. Wonder, too, why I love her, not every minute, but often enough so I never forget that, in fact, I do.

I know my child will probably never speak, that she will be handicapped and hard to control for the rest of her life, that she will be a financial drain forever. I also know that this morning she awoke with a smile, her blue eyes shining, her ponytails mussed from sleeping. I know that whatever she is to become, she is, at least momentarily, a source of pleasure to me. Strange that I am even proud of her for finally sleeping well.

[Later that day]

As we took a ride, she whooped and played in the back seat of the car. The sun was bright and warm for winter, the wind a little damp. She reached over the seat, as she often does, and hugged me around the neck, letting me know in her way that she was there and glad of it. I realized that an hour later she would be cranky again, and that a year later she would still be retarded. But I decided that it didn't matter, for this moment, because, well, it just didn't matter. There was a bond between us now, though it might be dissolved later.

CHAPTER 4

There didn't seem to be much doubt about it to me. Although Jennifer was improving at Operation Discovery, the gains were so limited for such hard work. Home behavior was getting worse.

Yes, Jennifer was retarded as well as deaf. I tried to talk to Rainelle about it.

"She's retarded," I said. "The cardiologist was right."

"If she's retarded, how can she figure out so fast how to undo all the latches we put up to keep her out of things?" Rainelle asked.

"I don't know, but I'm getting pretty tired of going to school all day, going to work every evening, and then not being able to sleep at night. We've got to do something."

"Like what?"

"I don't know that either."

"Well, you're a fine psychologist. Why don't you get on it?" Rainelle said.

"Look, don't give me that line. I've heard it before and it makes me mad. I'm just saying this has to stop."

"You're not the only one that's tired of things around here. But Jennifer's not retarded," said Rainelle.

"Okay, so what is wrong then?" I growled.

And so it went.

We had long since stopped trying to take Jennifer with us to visit friends (as if we had time for that amenity anyway with work, school, and doctors' visits). Jennifer couldn't be controlled, and the visiting created more trouble than it was worth.

"Let's go visit Gary and Jane," I said one evening.

"I don't feel like it tonight," Rainelle said.

"Why not?"

"I just don't want to."

"We never go anywhere anymore; I'm really sick of it, Rainelle," I said angrily.

"It's never any fun for me, George. I'm always the one who has to watch out for Jennifer; so I'd rather not go."

"That's not so," I said. "I watch out for her too. I just prefer to let her roam more than you do. She's got to learn sometime what she can and can't do."

"Sure, George, sure."

Friends and relatives never understood, I think, why we seldom brought Jennifer to visit. We tried to explain that Jennifer would wreck their house or wreck us keeping her from it. I certainly didn't explain how Rainelle and I quarreled about making visits to friends' houses.

Invariably, when we would hesitantly accept an invitation someplace, something valuable would get broken, and we couldn't just dismiss the damage by saying "we warned you." If we did manage to prevent damage from occurring, we were emotional wrecks from split-second dives to catch falling pieces of china.

Our hosts seldom sensed our discomfort; they would remark as we left, "See, Jennifer wasn't so bad after all."

There was no reply to such a remark, which seemed like another way of saying "it's all in your mind; you're making it up."

The real aftermath was when we returned home.

"See, you just don't watch her closely enough," Rainelle would say.

"Nothing broke, Rainelle. We just can't stop going places."

At home or away, there was the sound of china breaking.

It's hard to say just when I became aware of how little I could safely say to my friends and relatives about things at home. No one would want to listen to me complain about having to clean shit off the walls.

One day I took Jennifer to school with me, but I had to put her on a leash; otherwise she would run away. The comments of a secretary at school capsulized my inability to act in any manner without being criticized.

"Why have you got that little girl tied up like some kind of dog?" she asked.

"Because if I don't, she'll run away; and if I try to hold on to her hand, I can't do anything except concentrate on that."

Jennifer was running in circles, chafing at the bit.

"Well, I think that's cruel," said the secretary. "I never had to treat my children that way."

Rather than try to explain, I just left.

Many people were unintentionally and unknowingly cruel. One day during a work break several of us waiters, all college students like me, were sitting in the lounge. We complained about tips and, of course, the management. Chicken bones and cigarette butts littered the table. We made fun of customers to release a little hostility, and we traded jokes.

"Did you hear the one about Helen Keller falling down the well?" one waiter asked.

"No," I said.

"She broke six fingers yelling for help!"

I didn't laugh.

"That might be funny if my daughter wasn't deaf," I said, hoping to teach him a lesson.

His face flushed, and he apologized.

Later, I couldn't decide who had been the bigger

ass—he for telling the joke or I for not just politely laughing and letting it pass.

It was hard to share with my friends what I was going through. I didn't want to bore them with my problems, and I didn't know how to say what needed saying without spending several hours.

But the worst part was that I didn't dare tell everything. Some of my thoughts were just too evil.

For example, I had read about a bush whose leaves contained a chemical that caused heart failure. My fantasies were of crushing some of these leaves and feeding them to Jennifer, who'd had heart problems anyway. Who would suspect?

But what horrid person could even think such a thing?

I also used to amuse myself by imagining that kidnappers, in *Ransom of Red Chief* fashion, would apprehend Jennifer and face worse problems than even O'Henry could envision. I pictured Jennifer being told to sit still by some poor fool kidnapper who, as in the O'Henry story, would finally pay me to take her back.

I recognized in my fantasy a wish for the problem to be removed without my having to be responsible for it. Kidnapping would have been a guiltless way to get rid of my troubles.

But who would hear such a thing without condemning me? I didn't know whether Rainelle also had such thoughts. There were times when Rainelle was visibly angry with Jennifer, but she never acted on her feelings other than to yell at a little girl who couldn't hear anyway.

Jennifer continued school at Operation Discovery after the unchanged diaper incident. Her teacher was doing a great job of teaching her how to read a few simple words, but there wasn't any progress on the toilet training. I thought a four-year-old should be finished with that developmental stage.

57

Rainelle was still trying to complete her bachelor's degree in English and political science. I began to teach part-time at a community college as well as wait tables and attend classes. Rainelle was working at a restaurant to help pay the bills. It was not the same restaurant where I worked. Sometimes we were able to work the same shift, however, and Jennifer stayed with Rainelle's mother, Wilma. We were very busy, and we needed to get some relief from the onerous task of cleaning diapers.

Disgusted with the school's efforts to toilet-train Jennifer, I decided to do it myself. After all, my master's degree was all but finished, and I knew more now than I did when I tried to teach Jennifer to talk. Maybe this experiment would be a success. One of the classes I taught was educational psychology at a local community college. I decided to use my experiences with Jennifer to illustrate to the class the problems of behavior modification.

[Diary and Notebook, April 1974]

Jennifer is deaf, intellectually impaired, and energetic enough to shame an Arab Sheik, and she needed to be toilet-trained. I found an article on toilet training of the retarded (by a man named Philpot—appropriate name) and I decided to employ fair science for useful purposes.

The paper described behavior modification techniques and some nifty electronic gadgets designed to activate lights on the face of a clown when the subject urinated in a potty chair, which rang a bell to notify the experimenter that the desired deed had been done. He then could rush to the potty chair to "reward" the subject with a treat. Supposedly, the treat and the lighted clown "reinforced" the child for pottying correctly (increased the frequency of the behavior). Since the clown and the bell were activated when the current passed through the new water in the chair, I tried to figure out what would happen if the child merely had a bowel movement. I should have been suspicious.

Like a fool, I tried to build the magic chair by following the simple diagram. I needed only a few capacitors, batteries, light bulbs, and wire. I wired and rewired, and though I got some terrific bubbling action from it, the water in the chair never conducted enough current to light even a little bulb. It reminded me of the time I wired a banana to electrocute a nibbling rat; I ended up with a fried banana.

I decided that I didn't need a bell or a lighted clown, which was a cheap trick anyway. Instead, I just listened for the sound of splashing water. The procedure was very simple: every twenty minutes I took Jennifer to the chair for a five-minute interval. If she went, she got goodies. I recorded "successes," but they did not seem to be increasing rapidly. Obviously, I had not found the correct reinforcer. This I had not anticipated, because I was using her favorite candy, M&Ms. Regardless of how much she seemed to like M&Ms, she wouldn't work for them; I had to look for something else to use. Eventually I stumbled onto buttermints, which began to work and the "frequency" rose.

I luckily caught her several days in a row and guided her successfully to the potty chair, but the buttermints did not seem to have enough power to motivate her to do her messy business in the chair rather than on the floor. One day while Rainelle was baking, she opened a box of brown sugar, and Jennifer, as she often does, motioned that she wanted some. "Why not," we said, and from Jennifer's reaction we knew we had discovered brown gold; Jennifer would fight tigers for a spoonful of brown sugar. So we began to use it as a reinforcer for bowel movements, using buttermints for urination.

Simple, right? Not quite. I forgot to mention that, in spite of potty chair success, Jennifer wet her underpants every five minutes (I kept trousers off her during this part of the training), so now I began to reinforce her for having dry pants, or for not going. This was so effective that soon she went for a day at a time without going, which was a problem because she wouldn't wet even in the chair. Reducing the reinforcement for not going eventually solved this problem, but there were still others.

Another problem was teaching Jennifer to take herself to the bathroom when she had to go. To this point, she would go only when taken, so we began to reinforce her for going near to and eventually sitting on the potty chair.

The first time she took herself and urinated all alone, I thought I was home free. I happened to be wrong. Still, I wish I could describe the elation and satisfaction I felt at her complete success.

After several more weeks, Jennifer was going to the bathroom by herself much more regularly, though she continued to have lapses of control. Unfortunately, and I still don't know why, she didn't seem to understand that she was still supposed to take herself to the bathroom even when she had jeans on. Then I discovered that she couldn't pull her overalls down, so I began to teach her the trick.

I also had to teach her to pull her clothes back up when she finished, all without language. On many occasions Jennifer has gone into the bathroom fully clothed, only to emerge naked as a jaybird. There were times when Jennifer seemed to be regressing. My mother was convinced I would never succeed until I left diapers off the child at night. I never did understand her reasoning, but she claimed to be The Voice of Experience. An increase in "accidents" also seemed to be related to illness and temperatures or periods of excitement. Once, I was unable to find any reason whatever for Jennifer's poor performance. She seemed disinterested in the buttermints, unwilling to work for them, and lackadaisical about eating them when she did earn them. Then I discovered that her grandmother had a sack of them in the cabinet and handed them out like they were, well, candy. No wonder Jennifer wouldn't work for them at home.

There's one more thing I hadn't anticipated when this adventure first began. I eventually wanted to have Jennifer go to the bathroom without having to have a mint at the finish; so I began to give her mints only every two times she performed. This was a sound, well-established procedure, which incidently would, in theory at least, increase the behavior's strength. I didn't expect the overt rebellion, then subtle manipulation, that followed. The overt rebellion came the first time I omitted the mint. Jennifer held out her hand; when she didn't get anything, she went to the mint jar, pointed, and began to cry. It was never like this with the white rats. When this tactic failed, she quickly moved to better methods. If she was going to get one mint for every two performances, then she would just perform more often.

60

What bladder control she displayed! Every five minutes she went to the chair and released just enough water to wet the bottom of the chair. After all, fair is fair, and if I was going to be cheap with the mints, she'd just get cheap with the water.

Jennifer's toilet training was at least a partial success. But she was four-and-a-half years old and had very little language. We thought what she needed most now was communication—that and better sleeping habits. We began looking for another school.

Whether we would be able to afford the tuition for special schools was a real worry. I heard from a friend that the Easter Seal Society might pay for help for Jennifer. I wrote to its representative in St. Louis and received a reply in less than a week. I was referred to an office in Kansas City with assurances that something could be done. Just getting a reply in such a short time—not to mention the encouraging attitude—made me feel good.

The Kansas City Easter Seal office answered my inquiry in three days, recommending that a psychological evaluation might be helpful in deciding educational placement. We were instructed to choose a psychologist and forward the bill to Easter Seals. I cried when that letter came; it seemed like somebody finally really wanted to help. I was so sick of red tape and waiting in line.

We arranged an appointment with a psychologist in private practice who was recommended by one of my professors. The psychologist was a woman who specialized in children. Her office was a suite in a medical building and was expensively decorated. A fine antique desk was the highlight of the interviewing room.

The interview started with introductions and small talk and proceeded to questions.

"I see from these other reports that Jennifer is premature and has had heart surgery. Now you're concerned about her educational placement. What is it you wish me to do for you?" she asked.

"Well, we're trying to find a school for her, but we don't know of a good one that can help her with her language," I said. "Can you recommend one? And we'd like to know if she's retarded or what. I know something about testing but not enough to diagnose Jennifer. Besides, I'm just too close to her to be objective."

"You've had Jennifer at several schools already," the doctor said. "But something hasn't worked out in each of them, and you've withdrawn Jennifer. Can you tell me about this?"

Rainelle answered, "Yes, we withdrew Jennifer from the program in Columbia because we moved to Kansas City. The next program at the Kansas University Medical Center only lasted the summer. The preschool program for the deaf at the Children's Hospital had a thoughtless teacher who put headphones on Jennifer the very first day and scared her, so we took Jennifer to the Foundation School. They were good to Jennifer, but she started acting like all the retarded kids in her class. Besides, the teachers don't stay there long enough to establish any consistency. So we're taking her to Operation Discovery, but they're really not helping her language."

"I see," said the doctor. "Do you think Jennifer is retarded?"

"Not really," Rainelle said. "I mean, if you look at some of the things she can do, you'd have to say no."

"Mr. Harris, what do you think?"

"I don't know." I looked at the carpet and noticed a worn spot. "She's not retarded in the way I've learned about, but she sure has other problems. Anyway, that's what we're here to find out."

We then told the doctor about Jennifer's development: when she sat up, stood, and walked. We discussed her toilet training and sleeping.

Finally the doctor said she wanted to take Jennifer into another room to do the testing. Jennifer went without protest. They returned an hour later. That was all the work that could be done that day, so we scheduled another appointment.

We returned a week later. The doctor began by discussing the test results.

"Jennifer does test in the moderately retarded range," she began.

"Does the testing take into account her hearing problem?" I asked.

"Yes, to some extent. But even making allowances for that, she would still be in about the same range. I think you need to begin to make long-range plans for her future care."

There was a moment of silence. Then I asked, "You mean some kind of institution?"

"Yes, possibly," said the doctor. "But before we make too many plans, I'd like you to have Jennifer examined by a neurologist, a medical examination. He may be able to help with medication that could calm Jennifer some."

"Will Jennifer grow out of this?" I asked. "I mean, is it possible she tests retarded now but could do better later?"

"We don't know. All that can be said is that she is functioning as a retarded child now, and of course she's deaf."

As we drove home, Rainelle and I were disturbed.

"How could she make a statement like that when she was only with Jennifer an hour?" Rainelle said.

"That's what the tests are for," I said. "Anyway, let's go to the neurologist and see what he says."

It was a fitful evening for Jennifer; she cried throughout, refusing to be comforted, as if trying to break the spell of her silent world.

We took Jennifer for her electroencephalogram and, six days later, for her neurological appointment. We went to the doctor's office expecting very little to happen. Easter Seals, fast becoming my favorite charity, agreed to cover the charges for this examination too. It was certainly a pleasure to go to offices in medical buildings rather than in public clinics or hospitals. The waiting rooms were clean and lines nonexistent. I could even pretend I was paying for these visits myself, thereby retaining some sense of dignity.

Dr. Braun was very friendly. He greeted us, asked some simple questions, and began to play with Jennifer. He tapped a small rubber mallet to test Jennifer's reflexes; he looked in her eyes, ears, and mouth; then he measured the circumference of her head. When we returned to the main office, Dr. Braun found some toys for Jennifer to play with and assured us she would not be able to hurt herself or anything else. He asked us just to let her play while we talked.

"I'm afraid there's nothing much medical science can do for your little girl," he began. "She is retarded. I don't find any evidence of epilepsy. Just how much she will be able to learn to do depends a great deal on the kind of training she gets, though eventually she will probably have to be put in an institution. This kind of thing is very difficult for parents to live with."

We sat in very somber silence; only the sound of Jennifer playing could be heard.

"I will give you some medication to help her sleep," the doctor said, "but I don't know if it will help. Sometimes it does, but it may not for Jennifer. I also want you to look into the Regional Diagnostic Center. They can provide some short-term childcare relief, like for vacations. You could leave Jennifer with them for a couple of weeks. Later they will help place her."

We asked some questions about what had caused Jennifer's problems. The doctor speculated that an infection during pregnancy, probably rubella, had affected her heart, ears, and head. He said he was sorry and suggested that we see him again at the Children's Hospital, where he was on staff, because the costs were less there.

It was impossible to hate such a nice man, much as I

wanted to. In feudal times kings killed messengers who brought bad news. Now I understood why.

Medical Report: July 29, 1974
RE: Jennifer Harris
DOB: 12/2/69

Thank you for referring Jennifer Harris. I saw this little girl in the office on 9 July 1974. As you know, current concerns center about (1) possible epilepsy, (2) hyperactivity and difficulty in management, and (3) small head size.

According to her parents, Jennifer was born 12/2/69 with a birth weight of 3 lb. 2 oz., the product of a pregnancy complicated by pre-eclampsia in the mother as well as kidney infection one month before birth. She was born approximately two to three months prematurely and was hospitalized during the first three months of life. Congenital heart disease was diagnosed at birth and she was operated on for patent ductus at age 3 months. Deafness was suspected in early life for which she has been evaluated twice at the University of Missouri Medical Center at Columbia and more recently at the KU Medical Center. There has been some disagreement as to whether her hearing problem is of cerebral origin or of peripheral origin [that is, whether Jennifer's hearing loss is a result of damage to her nerves or outer ear]. Jennifer did not walk without assistance until age 2 years. There has been no speech development. She has had no serious illnesses or injuries.

Review of family history reveals one relatively distant relative with what sounds like congenital nerve deafness. The maternal grandfather's sister is a deaf-mute. She apparently is a bright woman, however, and finished college. There are no other children in the family.

At the present time Jennifer is said to sleep poorly. She goes through cycles of staying up late and getting up early. She takes no naps. At one time she was on Ritalin, by Dr. Steppes, and also on Atarax at one time. Neither of these appeared to help hyperactivity. She feeds herself without too much assistance, mostly with a spoon. She is able to undress, but is not able to dress herself well. She has previously been in the Operation Discovery School and at one time was in Foundation School. She is partially toilet-trained.

On examination, Jennifer is a cute little girl. There are no distinctive somatic features, though her fingers are rather long and thin. Head circumference is 41¾ in., which is at the 25th percentile for age, and weight is 30 lb., which is below the 3rd percentile for age. I elicit no response nor reaction to sound. Otherwise the classic neurologic examination of cranial nerve, motor sensory, and cerebellar function is normal. I detect no evidence of cataracts. Activity and behavioral patterns appear to be at about an 18-month level of development.

Electroencephalogram obtained in my office on 7/3/74 was normal.

Neurologic impression: (1) psychomotor retardation, probably profound, (2) microcephaly, (3) congenital nerve deafness.

I suspect, as others have according to the parents, that this young lady's difficulties are probably secondary to intrauterine viral infection. She has many of the features of the rubella syndrome.

I recommended to the parents that they become involved with the Kansas City Regional Diagnostic Clinic. The clinic can be of assistance with things like behavioral modification programs, toilet training, family relief or crisis intervention, as well as being of ongoing assistance to the parents with any and all problems related to her retardation.

I commenced Jennifer on Mellaril concentrate, 10 mg. 3 times a day, with instructions to the parents that they could increase the dose gradually at several day intervals until a dose level is achieved that satisfactorily reduces her aimless hyperactivity. They are not to exceed 100 mg. three times a day, however, until the child is seen again. I also explained to the parents that since her activity level and behavior are really appropriate to her developmental age, that medication *may not* effect any particular improvement.

Since these delightful young parents are both students, I recommended to them that we follow Jennifer for medication management in the neurology clinic at Children's Mercy Hospital. I will effect an appointment there for follow-up in approximately 6 weeks time.

Thank you for referring these very nice people.

P.S. I neglected to mention above that I really find no evidence of epilepsy in this little girl. Her EEG is normal and the occurrence once or twice a day of pauses or staring do not really sound convulsive. Children with neurologic problems of this type are, of course, an increased risk for seizure disorders and we will bear this in mind in following her. At the present time, however, she does not appear to have epilepsy.

Any illusions I held that Jennifer was just "going through a stage" were shattered. Though Jennifer had shown the ability to learn, she was still far behind in her development and would never catch up. It took effort to endure each new day; the hope was gone. It was as though we were in mourning for the lost hopes and dreams.

Rainelle cried over the little girl who would never sit and listen to nursery rhymes. Everywhere in the apartment we felt chilled and damp.

We had one more appointment with the psychologist who was looking for a school for Jennifer. We went not knowing whether she had found one. I had talked briefly with this psychologist by phone after the neurologist saw Jennifer. I knew that his report had reached her but didn't know what else she had uncovered.

"Hello, Mr. and Mrs. Harris. Won't you come in?" the psychologist said. When we were seated, she continued, "What more have you thought since our last visit?"

"Oh, not that much really," I said. "The neurologist gave us some medication for Jennifer, but it's not that effective."

"Well, I hope you can talk further with him about that," she said. "You know, often the parents need to talk about their frustrations when they have such a child. Mrs. Harris, I would like to encourage you to seek some professional guidance to help you adjust to this situation."

Rainelle stared angrily.

"I suppose you two have gotten together and think I've got the problem, huh? Well, I don't think so," said Rainelle. "You spend an hour with my child and say she's retarded and ignore all the things I tell you she can do for me that she didn't or wouldn't do for you."

67

"Now, Rainelle," I said, "that's not the point. It's just that there always seems to be something wrong with every school we find for Jennifer, and we've got to accept that nothing is going to be perfect."

Rainelle had supposed correctly. The psychologist and I had talked about Rainelle. I was already seeing another counselor at the university and wanted Rainelle to come with me, but she didn't want to. Today's recommendation was a set-up, and Rainelle was understandably angry.

Again, I heard the china breaking.

Rainelle seemed to have developed a mistrust of counselors and psychologists—a mistrust I shared in some respects given our experiences with professionals. And Rainelle certainly didn't lack the native intelligence to form her own solid opinions. I shouldn't have talked privately with the psychologist, though at the time I thought it was in the family's collective best interest. It just backfired.

The psychologist recommended a school for Jennifer. She finished the session by telling us about it. It was a private school located in the basement of a church, and it handled many different kinds of children. The psychologist thought it might be a good place to try for one more year while we decided if we could handle Jennifer at home.

It was worth a try.

CHAPTER 5

Rainelle was officially a senior at the university and seemed sure to graduate. She began talking about law school, a long-time ambition. I couldn't understand why she wanted to go. She said she didn't want to practice law but was sure there would be other uses for her degree.

"Rainelle, you just don't have a lawyer's personality," I argued. "You're not competitive, and that's what you have to be when you're a lawyer."

"But I don't plan to practice law," she said.

"Well, great, if you can find a way to pay your way through, that's fine," I said. "But don't expect me to work my way through school and then support you through school too."

"I wouldn't think of it, George. Why do you always act like I'm trying to take something away from you?"

"All I'm saying is that you haven't worked to put me through school, and I don't plan to pay your way so you can get a degree you won't use."

I didn't know for sure why Rainelle wanted to go to law school. In part she seemed to want the pride of being able to call herself an attorney. No one else in her family had even graduated from college. But then, except for my brother before me, no one in my family had either. Rainelle once said how much fun it would be to send a copy of her law school diploma to the dean of the college in Columbia who had refused to re-admit her.

Looking back, it's easier to see that Rainelle may have needed law school in part because I showed so little faith in her.

In any case, I didn't look forward to the continued financial struggle of both of us in school and Jennifer needing attention too.

Before Jennifer started at her new school, we visited the Regional Diagnostic Center recommended by the neurologist who saw Jennifer in July. The center was on Hospital Hill in Kansas City, an area with a mental health center, the old public hospital, and a dental school. The purpose of our visit was to do even more intelligence testing. We also wanted to see if the center could provide short-term relief with Jennifer; it was hard to find babysitters who could safely handle Jennifer, or who would agree to keep her even if they could.

The results of the tests were no surprise. Jennifer was retarded. The staff said that temporary relief could be provided. The possibility of permanent placement was discussed, but Rainelle and I had agreed to keep Jennifer at home for one more year.

No matter how hard I tried, each time Jennifer was tested I couldn't help hoping that this time would be different—this time someone would find what was wrong and fix it. When the test results were explained, inevitably, inexorably, there was disappointment and sadness.

Psychological Test Results, September 1974
Jennifer Harris, age 4 years, 9 months

Psychometric:
Evaluation with the Merrill-Palmer Scale yielded mental age 32 months and I.Q. 59. Further evaluation was not attempted on this date. The Vineland Social Maturity Scale was administered and yielded social age 2.4 and a social quotient 40.

Occupational Therapy:
Jennifer was administered the Denver Developmental Screening Test. She was very hyperactive throughout the testing session. Personal-social skills appear to be at a 24-month level. Jennifer can feed herself with a spoon but refuses to do so. She washes and dries her own hands and dresses herself. Jennifer is toilet-trained but has difficulty communicating her need to use the toilet when she is away from the home.

Fine motor skills are at a 22 to 23-month level. Jennifer built a four-block tower, imitated a vertical line, scribbled spontaneously, and demonstrated a pincer grasp. No age level was given for language skills, as Jennifer is deaf. She used unintelligible vocalizations during the testing session. She frequently pointed, and she is able to indicate "drink, eat, bye-bye, and come." Gross motor skills are at a 2½-year level. Jennifer can balance on one foot, jump in place, throw a ball overhand, and kick a ball forward.

Diagnosis:
Mental Retardation, Level Unspecified. Hearing Loss.

My parents took the news about Jennifer remarkably well. They commented that they didn't know how we had managed Jennifer so well to date. This surprised me, because all I remembered to this point was their saying "she'll grow out of it."

Jennifer became increasingly difficult to supervise and watch as she twitched and jerked her little frame helter-skelter in an endless buzz of activity. She and I were in the car one warm afternoon and stopped by the apartment to get a book I'd forgotten. The parking space was fifteen yards or so from our apartment door. Rather than bring her in with me, I decided to shut the car door and quickly get the book.

I ran inside, looked briefly at the mail on the table, and returned to the car.

The door was open; Jennifer was gone.

"Oh my God," I thought.

I started to yell for her, but quickly squelched that senseless act.

"Don't panic," I said to myself. "Where could she go? In the back of the apartment is the field. If she goes the other direction she'll stop and play at the playground; if I check the field first and she's not there, I will have time to run to the playground."

I prayed that my reasoning was correct. Past the playground or across the field, highways, those long serpents of concrete, waited to lure Jennifer into the path of diesel trucks that would sneak up on her until it was too late to escape.

I dashed to the field and, sure enough, there she was. The weeds were chin high to her; all I could see was her head bobbing up and down as she ran. Sighing with relief, I ran after her and caught her. I tried to find some way of expressing to her how much she had scared me, but she didn't understand. All I could do was shake my head to say "no, no, no."

I sat down in the weeds with Jennifer on my lap. I hugged her until my heart slowed and the metallic taste of fear left my mouth. I would have to be more careful in the future. Jennifer, unaware of my concern, made her characteristic hooting sound as she struggled to free herself from my grasp to continue her flight into the brush.

By this time in Jennifer's life I thought I'd heard everything: grandparents who just knew nothing was really wrong; grandparents who were just sure the magic operation would soon be available; doctors who said Jennifer would outgrow her problem. Wishful thinking is hard to counter. Usually there is a seed of hope that the reality of the situation is not as bad as imagined; parents, like grandparents, don't want their child to be handicapped. It's easy to hope against hope that the problem is imagined, temporary, or at worst a problem the doctors will fix.

When I finally became convinced that Jennifer's problems were serious, somehow there was guilt at thinking this when others still had hope—and increased isolation, too, because I hesitated to say what I knew.

Once a handicap or infirmity is confirmed beyond the point of denial, there's always the well-intentioned or perhaps neurotic friend or relative who says, "Well, God must have wanted it this way." I took it upon myself for quite some time to humor this kind of remark, but I still found myself angry. Angry because my child was handicapped in the first place, and angry because I didn't see why I should have to tolerate such ignorant remarks.

Often, I could see that the person making such a remark was just groping for something decent to say to make me feel better. Other times, the remark was made by people not for me but for themselves, to ease their own anxieties or show their "compassion." When the latter occurred, I often answered that I hoped God knew what He was doing. Some parents of "normal" children would talk in condescending tones about Jennifer, as though their "normal" children somehow made them superior.

It is difficult not to let your self-esteem and self-worth be connected with the condition of your child. This phenomenon can be observed in any hospital waiting room where the father beams proudly when his bouncing baby is shown through the window. "That's what I did," he thinks to himself, "that's mine, that's part me."

If that offspring is handicapped, it's difficult not to make that same connection. I don't believe mothers are like fathers in this regard. Rainelle never seemed embarrassed about Jennifer, though she was sometimes frustrated by her.

People who meet Jennifer for the first time and learn about her problem often begin to deal with their own fears of having a handicapped child, or their own feelings, yet unresolved, over a loved one with similar problems. Whenever people genuinely seemed to understand my pain, though, my eyes welled with tears that found no safe place to fall.

On many occasions Rainelle and I would describe

Jennifer's activity level to a physician only to have him or her smile paternally/maternally and say that all children tend to be more active than parents can handle. There was a great satisfaction in unleashing Jennifer on pediatricians who said such things. Watching them try to pin her down for an ear exam was delightful. One physician who had doubted us changed his mind when he saw her shins, bruised from climbing any obstacle before her; they looked like pears thrown off a cliff.

As the summer reached its muggiest period, an incident helped me to laugh at this problem a little. A chiropractor told my parents that one of his colleagues successfully treated hyperactivity and deafness through chiropractic manipulation. I didn't have much faith in such techniques, but we agreed to take Jennifer to see the chiropractor, partly out of curiosity, partly out of hope, partly out of my parents' offer to pay the bill, if necessary.

Rainelle, Jennifer, and I went for an interview during which the chiropractor explained the procedure, "cranial therapy." After aligning the spine, he would manipulate the bone in the head by massaging the insides of Jennifer's mouth.

I informed the good doctor that Jennifer would not allow her back to be "manipulated" and that, if he put his hands in her mouth, she would bite him.

He assured us he "had a way with children."

In the first session, he coaxed Jennifer onto his padded table and tried to get her to lie on her stomach. She wriggled and squirmed to keep her back away from the doctor.

"Now, Jennifer," he said, "I won't hurt you."

His tone was persuasive. I nearly jumped on the table myself to keep such effort from being totally wasted on deaf ears.

"It won't hurt," he said.

Rainelle looked at me and rolled her eyes. We both tried not to giggle. The first session lasted thirty minutes with lots of struggle and no "alignment."

I explained to the doctor my use of candy as a reinforcer in some behavior modification procedures. He laughed patronizingly and said I was only trying to bribe her. But at the end of the session he gave Jennifer some mints to get her to come to him. This was his "way" with children. He nearly convinced me that behavior modification would never work with Jennifer.

A few days later we returned for the second session. The doctor said he was sure that Jennifer had misalignments in her spine because her high activity level was bound to have caused some damage. When he began to turn her on her stomach, Jennifer pawed her way off the table and got underneath, where there were knobs and levers to control the angle and elevation of the table.

It looked like a Marx Brothers movie: Jennifer crawling under the table, pressing first this lever, then that, as the chiropractor tried to position himself to capture the trouble-making child.

"Don't push that lever, Jennifer," he yelled.

Rainelle and I finally laughed out loud and came to the rescue. This was how it went for another session or two. Finally he did try to look in Jennifer's mouth. She did bite him, and that was the last we saw of the chiropractor.

Jennifer was enrolled at the Children's Special Education Center in the fall of 1974.

Like many other programs for the handicapped in Kansas City, the center was private, even though tuition came from public funds. The public school system did not directly provide services for many children, so other groups had to fill the gap. Classes were held in the basement of an old stone church not far from the university. Although it was on the edge of a residential neighborhood with expensive, old Tudor-style homes, the church was next to a major road that was always full of traffic.

Jennifer's first week at the center was uneventful. Her teachers were young and enthusiastic, though they did not seem especially empathic to the problems Rainelle and I faced as parents. I suppose that, even though they were my age or a little older, they didn't have children of their own, much less handicapped children. They had no way to relate to our problems through personal experience.

For example, I had suggested that they try to teach Jennifer how to blow her nose into a handkerchief, a skill she had not developed. The teachers, however, spent more time on puzzles and games—important activities but not high on my list of priorities for Jennifer. It seemed that we weren't listened to as much as we would have liked.

When we enrolled Jennifer at the school, we were careful to explain her toilet habits, her eating preferences, and her tendency to wander or run away from supervision. Jennifer, I said, was the Houdini of playpens.

The teachers nodded politely but didn't seem to be as struck by the revelation as I had hoped. I didn't know how else to state my case to them without appearing to be a Cassandra. It was frustrating to watch them nod in agreement; it felt like condescending politeness. "Another exaggerating parent," I could almost hear them say.

Jennifer's first escape was the worst. She somehow got out of the school and went up the street. Fortunately, she headed away from the busy main road and into the residential district. An observant housewife saw her playing in the backyard and went to investigate. She wisely held on to Jennifer when she found that Jennifer couldn't talk.

After thirty minutes of frantic searching, the teachers spotted Jennifer and the housewife and went to the rescue. Sheepishly, and reluctantly, they told us what had happened when we came to pick up Jennifer.

The second escape a week later was less alarming. Jennifer's teachers had been securing the outside doors as a result of the first escape. This time they knew she was somewhere in the building. First they searched the basement of the large church. No success. They proceeded to the deserted chapel.

There was Jennifer, stripped entirely naked, cavorting across the altar, whooping in sheer delight.

Jennifer always seemed to dislike clothing or restraints of any form. She would take any opportunity to make a mockery of customs whose usefulness no one could explain to her. So there she was, defying not just a school but a church as well. I doubt she understood how "inappropriate" her behavior was; she was just having fun, being free. The next time I related a message about Jennifer, her teachers seemed more receptive.

After three months, the school reported Jennifer's progress.

Semester Report, 12/74

Social Skills with Adults:
Jennifer reacts to an adult when the need arises either by pulling on the adult's hand and pointing or by whimpering. She will respond much better now than at the beginning of the school year with her eye contact. She is generally following sign language better now than at the beginning of the year and will respond accordingly.

Social Skills with Peers:
Much of the behavior exhibited by Jennifer with the other children is in an aggressive manner. She seems to really enjoy the other children, but is not quite sure of how to approach them. She usually will give them a hair pull, pinch, or bite for their attention. This will usually get a quick reaction from the other children and she then smiles. We are trying to encourage appropriate bodily contact with friends, such as holding hands or gentle pats.

Gross Motor Skills:
Jennifer seems to really enjoy physical activities such as jumping, running, tumbling. She also likes to ride a tricycle during free play. She pedals well, but is not guiding the tricycle yet. She is doing better catching and throwing the ball.

Language:
Jennifer is non-verbal and does not respond to verbalization. She seems to understand and respond to limited sign language. She will imitate the ma-ma sound with sound. Other sounds she may imitate the lip action, but without sound.

Jennifer's conceptual skills are somewhat limited. She matches beautifully (Judy Matchettes, parquetry series, lotto games, colors and numbers). She can match colors and shapes as shown in the parquetry series. Puzzles pose few problems for Jennifer; when she needs help, she'll gesture with her hands. By matching with the parquetry blocks, she makes 2-D into 3-D. She has no trouble with the shape box or the play chips.

Jennifer's attention span has increased remarkably. She can complete a puzzle with no attention from anyone else. She also stays with a harder task with much less frustration. During play time she will stay with an activity for a much longer period of time. She doesn't flit around from one thing to another. Her frustration tolerance is still low and she will cry for a long while for no apparent reason.

Jennifer enjoys art immensely! She is holding a crayon by herself and she scribbles freely (she was unable to hold a crayon or draw with it without help in September). She also enjoys painting, especially at an easel. Jennifer likes fingerpainting and pasting, also. Her creativity is not particularly high, but she is exploring and experimenting with this medium. Music for Jennifer consists of playing the autoharp or other instruments and gross motor movements such as walking on tip toe, swaying, clapping hands or hitting her hands on the table. Otherwise, music is of little interest to Jennifer.

It was New Year's eve, 1974. I was thoroughly sick of being a waiter—so weary of it that I made a most uncharacteristic, impulsive decision. My New Year's resolution was that I would never spend another evening or weekend waiting on tables. For more than two years I had worked every Wednesday, Thursday, Friday, and Saturday evening and ten hours on Sunday. I went to the restaurant, uniform in hand, and resigned.

The feeling of freedom was wonderful. But I didn't have another job. I didn't know where the needed money would come from. Fortunately, within a few days I was offered courses to teach as an adjunct instructor at several local colleges. The pay was miserable, but it was something. Within a month, I also found a full-time job doing psychological testing in a vocational rehabilitation workshop. I was delighted to have my first 40-hour-a-week professional position.

I was clearly overloaded with work, but I didn't feel I could quit anything, including the three courses I was taking in graduate school. I worked and went to school from 8 a.m. to 10 p.m. Monday through Friday and had to study all weekend. I do not know if I stayed so busy to avoid being home or if my need for achievement was just operating at irrational full-steam. I do know that continuing all these activities was clearly a roadblock to establishing any sort of family life.

The winter of 1975 passed quickly. Days blended into one another; the routine of daily living seemed a continuous cycle of school, work, and nights of sleep broken by Jennifer's frustrated crying. The uncertainty of Jennifer's future loomed like a storm on a distant horizon, but we lived without much talk of how we could weather the squalls.

What was the nature of my little girl's problems? Would she ever be able to fit in with so-called normal people? Would they accept her or scorn her? Would she ever be able to communicate? As spring approached there were two events that made me think about this confusion.

I bought a van previously used by the Postal Service. With the steering wheel on the right, it was odd to drive. But I knew Jennifer would have lots of fun roaming around the cargo area. I planned to put carpet and cushions in it. First I had to get the van mechanically checked, so I took it to a garage.

I had to take Jennifer with me. Just the thought of corralling her while there made me tired. She was always excitable, but in new, strange places she was unmanageable. Unless I wanted to keep one hand on Jennifer at *all* times when we went somewhere, I had to look for a room with no breakable objects where Jennifer could play.

The garage had no such room.

As I sat waiting for the mechanic, with Jennifer squirming in my lap and making me nervous and irritable, I got an idea: The van could serve as a playpen. The tension in me eased with each step we took toward the "rolling cage."

The mechanic motioned that he was ready. I pulled the van inside where he could put it on the lift. By this time I was convinced that the cargo area was God's gift to parents of "hyper" children, and I decided to lock the doors and send Jennifer up with the van.

As it went up, Jennifer peeked out the windows, looking pleased and excited. She was having a ball. Soon she settled into the driver's seat where she energetically (what else) began to turn the wheel back and forth.

What was great amusement for Jennifer was hell on the mechanic, who nervously tried to dodge the twisting, turning wheels. I stood in the doorway chuckling to myself as my rapscallion found her way to wreak havoc even while on a lift.

The mechanic was a nice man. He patiently continued greasing the van, trying to dodge the tires. But then he needed to get to the grease fittings. He could not do so unless the wheels stopped moving.

"Little girl," he yelled, "you're going to have to stop playing there for a while so I can work, okay?"

Jennifer, oblivious to his sounds, continued playing Mario Andretti.

"Little girl," the mechanic shouted, "please don't do that, okay? See, I've got to finish this, okay?"

I was amused; I knew Jennifer couldn't hear, and I knew the mechanic didn't know it. I also felt good because Jennifer, to this mechanic at least, looked like any other little girl; I had become quite tired of thinking how different Jennifer was and having other people comment on it.

I wanted to tell the mechanic something to let him know his requests were in vain, but I hesitated. I didn't know what to say. I could say, "She has central brain dysfunction and doesn't respond to sound," but that was rather long-winded. I could say, "She's retarded," but that didn't really seem to explain things either.

What I really wanted to explain was that he could yell until his grease curdled, and Jennifer wouldn't respond. But if I said just that, he probably would ask why, and I still would need an "explanation."

I decided to tell him that Jennifer was deaf, even if that wasn't the truth or the whole truth. As soon as I did, he looked quite surprised.

"No wonder she didn't stop that," he said. "I was getting pretty frustrated."

"Let's see if she can turn it now," he said as he put his shoulder against the tire to brace it and proceeded to grease the rest of the van.

When the mechanic was finished, he lowered the lift. Jennifer shrieked in excitement as the ground drew near. When I paid the bill and got in the van, she hugged me joyously, like a child who had been on a scary roller-coaster ride and was now home safe.

As we pulled out of the garage the mechanic yelled, "Bye-bye, little girl," already forgetting that Jennifer couldn't hear.

Reflecting on the incident, it seemed that having a "diagnosis" for Jennifer had been helpful even if it wasn't accurate. The mechanic accepted the diagnosis and quickly adjusted his work. But I also thought how diagnoses can be like brands; they are hard to wear off. If inaccurate, they can cause problems, like keeping a child labeled "retarded" enrolled in a retarded classroom when he or she could and should do better. The diagnosis then becomes a self-fulfilling prophecy; people expect certain things from a child and the child adapts to meet the expectations.

This problem was familiar to me because Jennifer had been labeled a rubella baby and "everybody knows rubella syndrome includes retardation." So Jennifer was retarded because she was a rubella baby. But there was no clear proof that Jennifer was a rubella child; the rubella titer done when she was three was inconclusive. In part the rubella diagnosis had been deduced from her other problems: her heart defect, prematurity, and deafness. But the logic of grouping ailments into a syndrome to get a diagnosis, and then using the diagnosis to infer more ailments (retardation), never seemed tremendously sound.

I knew that labeling Jennifer "deaf" had been helpful at the garage, but I recalled other times when I didn't like Jennifer being labeled. Yet she was bound to be labeled in some way. Even her name was a tag that carried different emotional effects than alternatives like Mabel or Gertrude.

The second incident that made me think about Jennifer's possibilities happened one evening when Jennifer and I were home alone. She was playing upstairs but came downstairs looking for me. She grabbed my hand and began to pull as she always did when she wanted someone to come with her. I was tired and irritated. "Why the hell can't my kid talk like any other!" I thought, resenting this burden.

I shook my head "no." I was too tired to go with her. I refused in a situation where I usually assented.

Jennifer paused, then placed one hand out, palm down. Next, she moved her other hand, also palm down, under the first hand. Then she moved her bottom hand to point up.

I sensed immediately that she had lost something under her bed and couldn't get it out.

Both of us, laughing, raced upstairs to retrieve her toy.

Not only had Jennifer shown an ability to "visualize" an object at a distant location, but she had communicated that to me in a way I could understand. It was the first time she had ever done such a thing. I was thrilled to communicate even in such a small way.

Aside from some progress in communication, Jennifer made little other progress. Her teachers reported on several occasions that Jennifer lost all control. She had tantrums, lasting from five minutes to all morning long, in which she cried and threw materials with no apparent provocation.

I knew the time was fast approaching when I could not stand to live with her any longer.

"Rainelle, I don't know how much more of this I can take," I said one day. "Jennifer isn't getting any better, and I just can't keep getting up four and five times a night with her and cleaning up after her all the time. I'm worn out."

"Well, what do you want me to do?" Rainelle said. "You wake up before I do. I can't help that."

"I know that," I snapped. "I think it's time we discussed placing Jennifer."

"You know how I feel. You remember that institution in Gainesville we visited. I will not put my child there no matter what."

"I know. But maybe there are other places," I said.

"Sure—with people that don't care about Jennifer. She's not like those other retarded kids. You know she isn't. I don't care what that psychologist said."

"Look, Rainelle, I'm at the end of my rope. It's either me or her. You choose, but I have some rights here too. I don't feel like I live here except to make sure you don't lose any sleep. I'm fed up. Do you hear me?"

Rainelle looked stunned. She began to cry from anger and hurt. There was no consoling her.

I probably appeared resolute, but I wasn't. My stomach churned. I felt the guilt of Judas magnified by centuries of inadequate atonement. There was no one to understand. It was a decision without compelling moral cause. By what right could I expel my own child from my home? And who would not think me evil for doing so?

That night Jennifer was strangely quiet. As I lay awake listening for her sound, the silence convicted me of my crime.

My sentence, I saw, was to walk barefoot through the slivers and shards of china broken by my treason.

CHAPTER 6

In early April Rainelle acquiesced to my demand. We went to the diagnostic center to meet the person who could help place Jennifer in foster care.

While we sat in the lobby, an older woman, perhaps in her sixties, walked in with two obviously retarded men, twins. Their facial muscles were poorly controlled; their lips remained slightly parted and their tongues licked their lips frequently and awkwardly. The woman told the men to sit down, as if she were commanding children. In fact, she was.

The twins were her children, she told the receptionist, and she had come to seek help for them for the first time because she realized that her boys, now in their forties, would outlive her.

How long this woman had endured!

Soon after this, a secretary ushered us into a small office, the walls of which were concrete block painted in light green like a lavatory. The man behind the desk was someone I remembered seeing at graduate school. He didn't recognize me, and I chose not to identify myself as a fellow student. It had become my custom not to let teachers and doctors know of my educational background, because then I seemed to get different treatment. I thought I saw their true colors when they didn't know about me.

"Well, Mr. and Mrs. Harris, tell me why you're here," he began.

"We've just about had all we can take with Jennifer," I said, "and as we've discussed with the people here before, we'd like to find out what programs are available that might accept Jennifer."

"I see. You know, of course, that it's very expensive to do this kind of thing. Do you have the resources to pay for Jennifer's care?"

"No, not totally, I'm sure, but I'd understood there might be help from the state."

"Maybe, maybe," he said as he leaned forward on his desk. "But the state doesn't pay for babysitters for my children. Why should the state pay for yours?"

I was taken aback. All I could say was, "I don't know what you mean." Then I began to feel my anger at his condemnation of my request.

"Are you prepared to let your child become a ward of the state?" he asked. "When you sign the papers to that effect, you will no longer have any say in her future. Do you want to do this?"

"I don't know," I said, containing my anger. "It depends on the kind of place Jennifer would be sent. Last time they said there were small groups of children living with families that took care of them. We can't send Jennifer to a big institution."

"Perhaps that could be arranged," he said. "I'll arrange a visit for you at one of the homes and you can see what it's like. We'll meet again, after you've visited, to see if it meets your standards."

Rainelle and I left the meeting feeling a mixture of depression and anger. We were quiet. I couldn't believe I had heard what I'd heard. Who was this person to belittle us in this way? Didn't he have any understanding of how difficult it was for us to consider putting our child in a home? Or was he testing our resolve? No matter, my dominant reaction was anger.

He had struck a wound that no bandage could cover, that no defense could protect from attack.

We visited the family group home a few days later and were pleasantly surprised. The "parents" were a man and woman in their mid-thirties who lived in a large suburban ranch-style home. They greeted us, gave us a tour of the home, and introduced us to their children and foster children. Their own two children were quite normal, perhaps ten or eleven years old. One of the foster children was a Down's syndrome girl about four years old who sat sweetly in her "mother's" lap. The other foster child was less than a year old and had obvious deformities in the face and body.

"It's easier for us to care for these children than it is for the natural parents," the foster mother said. "We love the children, but we don't hurt when we watch them. It must be hard for you."

"How do you manage with the foster children plus your own?" Rainelle asked.

"Oh, my husband is a fireman and has an unusual schedule, and I like having the kids here. And we have substitute help so we can get away. It works out."

It was such a relief to see the foster parents with Jennifer. We explained her problems, and they said they would just have to see how she worked out, assuming that the diagnostic center approved the arrangements. They told us that we would be allowed to visit Jennifer whenever we wanted, except for her first month, when it was difficult for the children to adjust with parents around.

In the car on the way home, Rainelle said she could accept Jennifer's placement in the home. We both agreed that Jennifer might even get better care with them than with us. Even their home was nicer. And, after all, we would be allowed to visit.

We made the decision and drove home without looking back, as though afraid of being turned into salt.

A week later we went again to the diagnostic center to discuss our reaction to the foster home. There was a sense of relief in having made the decision. Arrangements were made matter of factly. Rainelle and I also decided that we would move to a new apartment immediately after Jennifer was placed, so we wouldn't be haunted by memories of her in our old home. It would be a fresh start for us, a chance to get to know one another again without the demands of Jennifer's presence. We anticipated going to movies and sleeping late occasionally.

We were twenty-three years old going on sixty, and it was time to rest.

In mid-May we prepared to take Jennifer to the diagnostic center for two weeks of observation prior to placement in the foster home. We packed her special dresses and favorite pajamas, decorated with the stains of spilled grape juice and assorted slippery foods. We gathered up her stuffed animals and put them in boxes for storage. Grandparents were finally told what was to happen. To my surprise they were sad but supportive. It seemed to be the right decision.

Jennifer went without fuss to the nurse waiting at the center. There was, of course, no way to explain to Jennifer what was happening. But I ached for a way to explain, wishing for her to understand, to assent, to forgive. We unloaded boxes and kissed Jennifer. We waved goodbye as the nurse led her down the hall; we listened to the clack of heels that echoed in our ears, keeping time to the pounding of our hearts.

The sound of the footsteps faded and disappeared behind a metal door that slammed shut loudly, as if to emphasize finality.

"Goodbye, pumpkin," I thought. "Be good, Pitiful Pearl."

A week of loneliness and adjustment followed. The new apartment was like a silent tomb, yet I felt more at peace than I had for years. Rainelle also seemed calm. We talked about the change in our lives, concluding that we would just have to adjust and give ourselves time. At the time I didn't realize Rainelle's misgivings about our decision, and I didn't make any special efforts to console her. I wish I had been able to do that.

We were allowed to visit Jennifer at the diagnostic center the first Saturday after her admission. With eager anticipation, we entered the main building and walked to Jennifer's ward. The ward had a large dayroom with a television in the corner opposite a nurses' station, which was on a platform enclosed by plate glass. Jennifer was playing by herself near some chairs that lined one wall.

I fought hard to keep from rushing to her, knowing that Rainelle would want immediately to touch her little girl. Then a feeling enveloped me: This was not my daughter. She looked like Jennifer, but it wasn't Jennifer. I recognized her, but I didn't recognize her.

"That's not how my Jennifer picks up a toy," I thought, "and that's not quite how she walks."

Jennifer looked up and spotted us. I wanted her to run to us with arms open, to grab us and hug us joyously.

Instead, she stared momentarily, then resumed playing. Now that was Jennifer—aloof as ever. There was a certain comfort in this greeting. Rainelle walked to Jennifer, picked her up, and hugged her. Jennifer finally returned the hugging.

We stayed for more than an hour with Jennifer. The nurses said that she was doing just fine and that she seemed happy and bright. Yes, she was eating well. No, she didn't like the medicine being given to calm her. Yes, the observation and retesting were going fine.

We departed with a sense of relief. The decision had been sound. Jennifer was in good hands.

There was no reason to feel guilty any longer.

Several days passed uneventfully. Then one evening the phone rang. It was the director of the diagnostic center.

"Mr. Harris, I need to see you and your wife, sometime in the next day or so if possible."

"Is something wrong?" I asked.

"Well, no, not really, but we do need to talk. Will Friday be all right?"

I agreed to the appointment and told Rainelle. We wondered what the suspense was all about.

Friday came. After greetings and handshakes, the director ushered us into his office and closed the door.

"We've had Jennifer here for nearly two weeks," he began. "She's a very unusual little girl. We've had our psychologists test her again, and the doctors have also evaluated her. It seems we made a mistake when we diagnosed her previously. Jennifer is not retarded after all. She tests in the low normal range."

He paused and waited for our reaction.

Rainelle and I looked at each other with furrowed brows. We turned back to the director.

"What happens now?" I asked. "Rainelle never really thought Jennifer was retarded. I only know it's hell living with her. Does this mean she can't be placed through the agency?"

"Yes, that's right. She isn't eligible for our services because she has to be retarded. You get to take her home for now, and we're going to recommend that she be placed in the state school for the deaf. She would live there in a dorm; that should be enough structure to help manage her behavior. We hope that she'll mature and become easier to manage as she gets older."

He paused, then said, "What do you think about this?"

Rainelle bubbled her approval.

"Can we get her now?" she asked.

I was confused and wary. Jennifer hadn't changed in two weeks just because her diagnosis had. She wouldn't be any easier to live with, even if she wasn't officially retarded. But maybe she could grow up to be normal except for her deafness, if in fact it was really deafness. Maybe more time was what she needed.

With a mixture of happiness and anxiety, we went to get Jennifer. This time she ambled over when she saw us. She hugged us, and I thought she smiled. We picked up her toys and clothes, and we took her home, new diagnosis but same old grape juice stains.

Diagnostic Center Report, May 1975

Jennifer Harris is deaf and mute. She is very wiry and hyperactive. She does not accept commands that she can understand (by using signs). She is very stubborn. She does not interact with other children and shows affection very seldom.

Jennifer is toilet trained but cannot dress herself completely. She eats very well, but very slowly feeds herself. She cannot brush or comb her hair.

Diagnosis:
Intellectual: Not mentally retarded
Profound Sensory-Neural Hearing Loss

Recommendations:
1. Due to the fact that the child seems to be in need of a structured residential placement that would afford her the most appropriate educational program, it is recommended that she be referred to the Fulton State School for the Deaf for enrollment in their residential/educational program.
2. Due to the fact that the child is not mentally retarded, she is not eligible for services from the Department of Mental Health, Division of Mental Retardation and Developmental Disabilities.
3. Jennifer be dismissed to her parents.

Jennifer looked surprised when she arrived at our new apartment, a two-story duplex with huge oak trees in front and a large open park in back. There was a basement but no partitions anywhere to serve as barriers. After all, we had no plans for her ever living there.

I had decided that if life with Jennifer were to be tolerable, I would have to institute a get-tough policy on her sleeping habits. Most children seem to learn fairly quickly that mommy and daddy feel like strangling their little angel who wakes them at 2 a.m. I'm convinced that interrupted sleep is a leading factor in child abuse.

"What caused you to tie your child to the bed and stuff a rag in her mouth?" I could imagine the social worker saying.

"My child gets up at night," I reply unconvincingly.

I knew something had to be done. None of the medications had worked, from the amphetamines normally used on hyperactive children to the zombie-producing potions for retarded children. Besides, we hated the thought of drugging her. Rainelle was especially opposed to the use of medication on Jennifer.

Medicine was never easy to give to her anyway. She wouldn't swallow pills, and when we put smashed and powdered pills in apple sauce, apple butter, and mashed potatoes, she always noticed. You name it, we tried it. Because a spoonful of sugar is supposed to help the medicine go down, I even offered her sugar for taking her medicine. But this, like everything else, didn't work either. Eventually, we just gave up.

The attitudes of physicians and nurses about medicine for Jennifer were interesting. Most didn't seem to realize the pressure we felt to do something, anything, to restore calm in the house; nor did they realize the guilt we felt at using medicine to achieve this. Most people also seemed to disbelieve how difficult it was to get medicine down the throat of such a scrawny little girl—until they tried it themselves.

Looking back, I think it would have been easier for me to take tranquilizers or alcohol to calm down and not be so bothered by Jennifer, but I never did. It does not surprise me, though, that other parents often do, if only to sleep and escape for a few hours.

With Jennifer home from the diagnostic center, I remembered all the things she did at night that bothered me. A few months before the move to the new apartment, Jennifer had begun to laugh insanely at night. She awoke giggling and reached a shrieking crescendo. I always wondered, but never found out, why.

Jennifer's room had large windows, which was nice except when a full moon was shining directly into the room. Jennifer, howling like a she-wolf, then sang her homage to the silver orb for hours on end.

Why not pull the shades? Because Jennifer would tear down any shade she could reach in order to play by the light of the silvery moon. For lack of alternatives, we tried to ignore her noise.

Jennifer also would roam the house, finding trouble to get into. So it became necessary to put an outside lock on her door. She still made her presence known. It's rather difficult trying to ignore a child who beats on her door for thirty minutes, then, failing to get her way, sits in the middle of the floor reading comics by moonlight and streetlight, shrieking laughter at every page.

It was eerie. I didn't know how to make her sleep. Her behavior was strange, incomprehensible, and very irritating.

My get-tough policy was to remove even the slightest reward or attention Jennifer received for getting up at night. Her room had a large walk-in closet in which I placed a large cardboard box. Thereafter, when Jennifer began making noise at night, she was confined to the uncomfortable container. She finally learned to keep down the racket. Though the problem was by no means solved, things got better. At least there was something I could do to make me feel less helpless.

Why hadn't we done this before? Because locking your child in a closet so you could get to sleep isn't your everyday, Dr. Spock response. How would we explain why we did it? How could an outsider begin to understand our feeling that we'd had all we could take? Imagine: "So,

Mr. Harris, you lock your kid in a closet at night, do you? Your neighbors have reported hearing the child cry all night. It's no wonder. I would too if I were treated like that. You ought to be ashamed."

Even if nobody asked, there's a need to tell friends about your troubles and attempted solutions—but you can't. They might not understand; in fact, they might gasp their disapproval. So you say nothing and hope it all works out, because you know it will just have to, that's all.

I look back on that summer as a time of change for Jennifer and for me, but it's not really clear what in fact changed. Had Jennifer begun to sleep better because of my get-tough policy or because she had been sent away from home for two weeks and, somehow, realized she'd better straighten up? Or is it possible Rainelle and I were shocked by the loneliness and emptiness of a house without Jennifer and we now approached her with more purpose and resolve?

Whatever the explanation, I clearly remember that summer as the time I began to feel joy in the love for my child. When she came into a room, I more often wanted to smile than yell.

She was still an awesome, even burdensome responsibility. But before she had been a duty imposed on me from higher authority. Now I felt more satisfaction in giving, not just relief from discharge of obligation.

[Diary, August 1975]

Jennifer has a rather strange habit of refusing to sleep in a bed. She used to prefer rocking herself to sleep on the carpet, where she would quickly return if we had the audacity to pick her up and put her in bed. For a while, there was a large throw pillow she'd sleep on, but it was impossible to put protective sheets on it and, because of Jennifer's imperfect toilet habits, it acquired a rather strong urine odor. I felt like a creep having my little girl sleep on it, but she didn't seem to mind. Now that Jennifer has her own bed and sleeps in it, she still refuses to do it right. She turns herself around so her feet are at the head of the bed and her head is at the foot. No matter how sound asleep she is, if you try to turn her, she sleepily scrambles around to get back, as if pulled by a magnet.

Her behavior is a combination of Carlos Castaneda and the "contrare" in Dustin Hoffman's movie, "Little Big Man." The contrare was the Indian who was destined to do everything backwards. For example, he walked through underbrush backwards rather than use trails. When he wanted to wash, he patted himself with dust. Castaneda, studying the behavior of Don Juan, a Mexican brujo, spent hours trying to find his "power spot" on the front porch of a house. The mystic Don Juan had told Carlos that the power spot was the only place to be protected from the "allies," the foreboding supernatural forces. Combining those characters, Jennifer seems to seek her power spot in her bedroom by circling for several minutes (like Carlos) before placing herself backwards (like a "contrare"). Now that she sleeps better at night, who am I to argue.

Unfortunately, Jennifer seems to be expanding her repertoire of contrare behaviors. Now, when we want to get up early to go on a trip, she is impossible to waken; when we want to sleep in, she's up with bells on at 6:00 a.m. Like a true contrare, a sonic boom doesn't stir this little deaf girl of mine, but just let me pop the tab on a can of Coke and watch her come running from the soundest of sleeps. Perhaps, I wonder, can little contrare deaf girls smell Coke?

One night at bedtime, Jennifer was lying in her bed; as often happens, she was rocking back and forth, not gently, but vigorously. This seems to be her way of putting herself to sleep, as if attempting to drain her last ounce of nervous energy before sleep. As I watched her, I couldn't imagine what it would be like to be wound up like an eight-day clock, full of this tension that fights rest.

Jennifer was freshly scrubbed, with the scent of soap on her and on her clean nightgown. I turned off the lights and knelt by her bed. Sometimes, there's no predicting when, she will stretch out her arms for me to hold her. Tonight she did, and we rocked together until she was asleep. I found myself trying to imagine what her experience of life was like.

Though the diagnostic center had recommended the Missouri State School for the Deaf for Jennifer, the school was in Fulton, a three-hour drive from Kansas City. Having just gone through the stress of placing Jennifer away from home only to have that stratagem fail, we couldn't go through the trauma again. The administrators at the school for the deaf were not that thrilled about having Jennifer either. When we visited the school, the administrators reviewed her file and interviewed us. All of us thought that another year at home would be best for Jennifer.

Rainelle and I talked and agreed that we could probably work things out, though I was still more hesitant than Rainelle. My interest in computers had waned, and my job doing psychological testing in a rehabilitation program made me begin to wonder if there was anyone anywhere who wasn't handicapped. Many of my clients had brain tumors that left them partially sighted, spinal defects that paralyzed their limbs, or diseases that atrophied facial muscles into grotesque expressions.

Many nights after work I would drive by the Plaza in Kansas City, a fashionable shopping district, so that I could see whole bodies, trim and well-kept. Without this exposure to the other side of life, it was difficult to keep perspective on what was normal human anatomy. So my schedule took me from work to graduate school to home. It was hectic but manageable as long as Jennifer was reasonably well-behaved.

Rainelle graduated from college and applied to law school but was turned down. She was disappointed but determined to study hard and retake the entrance exam. She took a job as an editorial assistant for a small trade magazine and decided to re-apply to law school the next year. Rainelle was always very good with languages and writing. We thought her job would be good experience, and it would give us some financial stability. Though not flush with money, some of the financial pressures of earlier years receded.

Our main concern was finding the right school for Jennifer. The staff at the Children's Special Education Center said they couldn't help Jennifer much more than they already had. They recommended that Rainelle and I check into the Sherwood Center, another behavior modification program primarily for autistic children.

Autistic children are perhaps the most perplexing of problem children. Often quite intelligent, they are withdrawn, sometimes self-destructive, and always hard to place educationally. Though Jennifer had some autistic-like behaviors (rocking motion, fascination with lights), she was not autistic. Nevertheless, we allowed her to go to school there because there was nothing else to try for the next year.

Fortunately, the classroom to which Jennifer was assigned had perhaps the perfect teacher for her at that time. A strict disciplinarian, Kathy tolerated no disruptive, bizarre behavior—which can be a problem in a classroom where children have been known to chew on their own flesh. She wore her hair boyishly short and her clothes with little concern for anything but comfort. Blue jeans and a shirt, always clean, were as fancy as she got.

Jennifer seemed to blossom under Kathy, whose manner was a classic display of tough love. Kathy studied sign language after school hours in order to pass it on to Jennifer. No parent could ask for more dedication. Kathy soon had Jennifer matching pictures with both the written word and the proper sign at a faster rate than I ever thought possible. Jennifer sat until allowed to stand and worked until allowed to play. Well, most of the time anyway.

When I dropped off or picked up Jennifer at school, other parents, usually mothers, were there doing the same. Sometimes we talked briefly, but it depressed me. It made me realize how difficult life was for the parents.

"Oh, yes," one mother said, "John has to wear that football helmet all the time, because it doesn't hurt him as bad when he smashes himself into the wall."

Another mother had two autistic children, no husband, little income, and a beat-up old Chevy that rocked and vibrated as if it had automotive heaves. I chose to believe it was the car, and not her situation, that had jolted her into her state of insensibility. Everything was inappropriately funny to her. She giggled when her car died; she belly-laughed when she ran into the curb. Her gaze was unfocused much of the time. I never saw her look like she was angry or, for that matter, like she was really in touch with the rest of the world. Her purgatory was to chauffeur her autistic children, stopping only to let them off, pick them up, and get just enough gas to make it to the next destination.

It was all really getting to me. But Jennifer, meanwhile, was making progress.

Academic Summary, March 16, 1976
Jennifer Harris, age 6

Jennifer currently has a signing vocabulary of 175 words. One hundred fifty of them have been formally taught. The words include 110 nouns, 32 verbs, and 12 colors. She currently uses two sentence forms: "I want _____" and "That is _____" to request and label.

She has been taught to follow 32 signed commands and is able to answer 11 general information questions.

Jennifer is able to read the numbers from 0–25, and is counting from 1–25. She can count up to 10 objects. In writing, she is currently working on copying the lower-case alphabet.

Jennifer acquires academic skills quickly, plays appropriately with others, and works for smiles, praise, and tickles, as well as food reinforcers. She is timed-out for any inappropriate behavior; her primary decelerative targets are teeth-grinding and whines.

We enjoy working with her. Jennifer is bright, fun, and usually a very charming child.

As the school year came to a close, it was apparent that Jennifer would again have to change schools. Kathy could learn sign language only so fast. Jennifer was far ahead of the other students in her class and wasn't learning much from being around them. It seemed that we'd never find a place where Jennifer could stay for more than a year. Getting to know a new school and a new teacher and new expectations of us were always a source of anxiety.

"Where do you think Jennifer will be able to go next fall?" Rainelle asked one evening.

"It doesn't look like she'll be able to go back to Sherwood, does it?" I said. "Maybe we ought to try the deaf school again."

"But Jennifer would have to stay in the dorm, and she still doesn't sleep that well at night. She would bother the other children, and they'd send her home. We'd be right back to Start again," Rainelle argued.

"Maybe, but maybe not. She really needs to be in a class with other deaf children, and there isn't anything in Kansas City," I said.

"You just don't want her living at home," Rainelle said angrily, "so you're trying to find someplace to send her away again."

"That's not true, Rainelle. I want what's best for all of us," I said. But her words were pointed arrows. They were impossible to pull out, and every rub against them was an irritant.

CHAPTER 7

Rainelle had retaken the law school entrance exam and gotten a score that better reflected her ability. She re-applied to law school and was accepted! She was elated and looked forward to starting classes. After some of the enthusiasm waned, ever-rational George sounded a cautionary note, which to Rainelle must have sounded threatening.

"It's great, Rainelle," I said, "but how are you going to find time to study? And how are we going to pay for law school? I'm already working full-time. They won't let you work at all when you start law school. It's too heavy a load. Jennifer's better at night, but she's still a lot of work. How are we going to do all this?"

"I don't know," she said. "I'll work, get loans, or do something. If you can go to school, why can't I?"

"Look," I said exasperated, "I'm pulling my share, and I won't do anymore. If you want to go to law school, you've got to figure out some way to do it."

"I will," she said, hurt and defiant.

Several days passed before we talked about this again, or said anything besides pass the salt.

"I've been thinking, Rainelle," I said. "If Jennifer stays

at school during the week, you'll have, we'll both have, more time to study and work. Jennifer can come home on weekends and we'll all be much better prepared to be with each other. Rainelle, you know that's the only chance you stand in law school."

Logic prevailed; Rainelle was sensible.

"Okay, we'll try it," she said, "but I don't want to."

Sometimes logic isn't very sensible.

We took another trip to the Missouri School for the Deaf to talk with the superintendent about enrolling Jennifer. Before the trip, we filled out the usual stack of applications and gave permission for release of information from what seemed like scores of previous schools, clinics, hospitals, and doctors. That was a full-time job in itself.

The school for the deaf in Fulton is adjacent to a state mental hospital constructed, it appeared, about the time Lee surrendered to Grant. Fulton has a very sleepy, small-town quality, perhaps because it is a sleepy, small town. My brother had been a pharmacist there at one time, so I was familiar with the town.

Our interview was in the administration building, a massive brick building that looked like one would expect a brick school building to look — solid but needing remodeling, with strictly institutional furnishings. The day was warm, but the building inside retained the evening coolness. It was quiet, and I imagined that the halls, instead of echoing the voices of a hundred years of students, would reflect the shadows of their hands as they talked in silent sign language.

The superintendent greeted us and ushered us into his office.

"Well," he began, "this is Jennifer."

Jennifer, recklessly, had moved from inspecting his desk to examining his bookshelves.

"She's certainly an active little girl," he said as Jennifer knocked a shelf to the floor.

After a few minutes of conversation, it was apparent there was some reluctance to accept Jennifer into the school.

"Jennifer was recommended to go here last year by the Regional Diagnostic Center," I said. "Is there a problem of some sort?"

"Perhaps. We're not sure we can manage her behavior here. For example, at night we may have only one person on duty. She could sleep in the infirmary, where there's more supervision, but that would pose a lot of problems and it would separate Jennifer from the rest of the kids."

"Maybe she could try that and gradually move into the dorm," I suggested.

"Well, I suppose we *could* give it a try," he said.

"It doesn't sound very certain," Rainelle said, "and I don't want to start this just to have to take her home in October and find something else."

"We can only say we'll try," the superintendent added. "We'll do our best."

We decided to take our one option—to give it a try. But we were uneasy and even resentful that no option seemed really good.

Rainelle wished out loud that there were some way to keep Jennifer at home. "She needs a home and parents," Rainelle said.

But there wasn't a way to do it.

We passed the time until Jennifer started school by making our own plans for the new school year. I took a new job working as a counselor for inmates in the county jail. Rainelle prepared to go to law school. I planned to continue taking courses at night toward my doctoral degree. There was no shortage of things to do.

But there was a curious silence in the house, a silence that even Jennifer's racket could not subdue. I talked little about my new job. Rainelle talked sparingly about law school.

We were busy in our silence as Jennifer's departure approached fatefully. Finally it arrived.

[Diary, September 1976]

Jennifer went away today to a residential school for the deaf. I felt such a mixture of sadness, nervousness, and anticipation watching my little scrawny kid walk away from me. I felt happy seeing what progress she had made overcoming huge handicaps just to get to try the school for the deaf, but my mind wouldn't let me forget the awesome task she had in front of her. I didn't even know if she felt uneasy in her new environment with new people; Jennifer still can't communicate such things. My stomach was tight and tense just thinking of all the trials, lumps, and bumps in store for my little baby. Later, I cried in private; it's getting to be a habit. I ached to protect her from an experience she had to go through.

I thought that here was an example of life throwing unsolvable contradictions at people. I wanted her in school; but I didn't want to let her go. I was immensely proud of my baby who had already overcome so many hurdles; but I was sad thinking why she had to have them in the first place. I thought about my wife and me who have struggled with this helpless little offspring, sometimes like horses in harness with different directions in mind. I reflected that it was just amazing how such a child could become the center of my feelings, the joy of my life. At the same time I knew that if I had it all to do over again, I wouldn't. I wouldn't subject the child to the things she had been through or would go through, and I myself wouldn't want to go through the agony and heartbreak of even the first year of her life. Still, Jennifer's good morning hugs and kisses are irreplaceable. How can that be?

The quiet in the house tonight with her gone is overwhelming. Though she irritates the hell out of me with her racket when she's home. I'm painfully lonesome now as I write this. I want to call her school to see how she is. I want to get in the car and drive the three hours to her school, even if just to catch a glimpse of her playing. I want to know that she's safe and that she knows she hasn't been deserted by us. I hope she makes friends. I hope she's happy. I hope she eats. I hope she gets hugged in the morning.

Will it always be so hard?

It's funny how apparently unrelated things seem to tie themselves together. I continued to be interested in Carlos Castaneda's books about the Mexican brujo, Don Juan. He was the mystical figure who took Castaneda as an apprentice in order to teach him to "see" the universe with supernatural vision. One of the tasks Castaneda had to master was to control his dreams. Don Juan instructed Carlos to learn to see his hands in his dreams. When this could be commanded at will, special powers would be at his disposal.

I was already fascinated with dreams and had kept a notebook of night visions for more than a year. I wondered if I could will an object like hands into my dreams. So I began to notice hands. Some were long and graceful; others short and awkward with hair on the back. Sometimes there was hair above the second finger joint; sometimes above the first joint too. But I never noticed hair above the first joint without there also being hair above the second joint.

One of my medical student friends told me that pranksters in medical school would cut fingers off cadavers and put them in coat pockets. Few practical jokes were as effective at getting shivers of revulsion, as though the human spirit still contained in these appendages was now reaching from the beyond.

We all notice different things. My dental student friends were obsessed with teeth. A well-constructed crown sent them into paroxysms of delight. There's no accounting for taste.

As I spent time with dreams and with criminals, Rainelle began to spend her time with law school, studying contracts and property law. With Jennifer in school, there was more time to explore our separate interests.

But where were our common interests, I wondered. Instead of taking time to talk about such things as dreams with Rainelle, I spent more time at school where there were people who shared my interests. I began to resent going home; I wanted to talk about this, without knowing what to say. After all, I'd had my way. Jennifer was in a residential school and would come home on weekends. What more did I want?

"Rainelle, we need to talk," I said.

"Okay. What about?"

"Well, I'm just unhappy with things. I mean, we don't do much more than live in the same house," I said as I thought how unaware she was of my tenseness. "And we've had this problem for a long time."

"We've been pretty busy, but what do you want to change?" she said.

"I don't know exactly," I answered, thinking to myself that it would help if we made love once in a while. I continued, "Besides, why is it always up to me to find the answer? I tried to get you to go into counseling with me so we could get some help, but you didn't like it; so it's your turn now to suggest something."

"Sure, George, blame it on me. That counselor we tried was awful. You had her number for sure. I felt like it was two against one, and I don't think that's right."

"All right. All right. Look, we aren't enjoying each other's company and we never sleep together anymore. We've still got problems," I said. "You always seem to have forgotten to take your pill, or something comes up that keeps us from sex."

"George, I am tired of this argument. It comes up over and over. I've told you I'm busy with school and I'm tired.

And about the pills, you don't want me pregnant again either. Just think how we'd get along with another child. . . . We don't even know for sure if it would be normal. We can't take chances."

There was a long silence as I stared at the floor, defeated, with nothing resolved.

Rainelle clearly felt little attraction for me. Though I felt the problem was in me, I acted as though it were in her. That's probably how she experienced things too, but neither of us could admit it.

"Okay, just forget it," I said.

That night I dreamed about a black, whirling tornado, hovering ominously above the horizon. Its center, its eye, was filled with the crackle of lightning that flashed back and forth discharging its dangerous energy. In the morning, I told only my notebook that I knew I had to leave.

A week later I confronted Rainelle with my decision. She argued that I shouldn't create this extra pressure on her during her first semester of law school. I said I just couldn't stand to stay any longer. The thought of divorce had occurred to me many times before, but it was never really an option while Jennifer lived at home. Jennifer was just too much for one person to manage; she needed too much supervision.

Rainelle cried. This was agony for me to see, but I didn't change my mind. The separation began a month later when I found an affordable apartment.

The apartment was as depressing as the circumstances under which I moved in. The kitchen cabinets were even painted black. But it was a place I could call my own, something I never had before in my life.

Many nights I sat alone wishing I had never been so stupid. Yet I knew it was necessary to live apart, at least for a while. We needed time and space to think.

Twice a month, Rainelle and I got together to bring

Jennifer home and to spend time with her. Jennifer visited my apartment, but it didn't seem to register to her that mother and father weren't spending nights together. Just how much she understood about anything had been an enigma since the day she was born.

Describing her is like trying to grab a will-o'-the-wisp. Her behavior was always so erratic. One day she would tune into the world around her; the next day she would ignore warnings of danger as if she were devoid of common sense. As many psychologists demonstrated by their conflicting opinions, Jennifer fits no precise category. No label exactly fits her.

Take her intellectual skills, for example. Although Jennifer was described at different times as both normal and retarded, these tags just didn't describe her. From a very early age Jennifer was able to show the ability to match colors with ease and put together jigsaw puzzles at or above her age level. Her major deficit seemed to be the adaptation of her intelligence to social development—a deficit not uncommon among deaf children, but one exaggerated in Jennifer.

I marveled at Jennifer's lack of shame, guilt, and empathy in social encounters. She felt no shame, as far as could be detected. During toilet training Jennifer never developed any detectable embarrassment at having messy pants; consequently, she could not be motivated to do better. Knowing what was expected of her, she would not only do the opposite but do it without any sign of guilt. On many occasions I would mimic hurt or disappointment with my best theatrical expressions only to have Jennifer giggle and laugh, unconcerned at my attempts. Sometimes she would even point her finger at me and mock me to other people, all in good humor, of course.

When I have explained this phenomenon to friends who do counseling, many have naively remarked how wonderful it is for a child not to be burdened with the silly restrictions of society. They would think differently if they had to clean four years of dirty diapers.

Perhaps also due to her shortage of guilt, Jennifer sometimes had problems restraining her impulses. For example, if Jennifer was sitting, I could place a toy or treat on a table and ask her to wait until I said it was hers. Most children above the age of six or seven could wait for increasingly long periods of time. But Jennifer, although she intellectually understood it was necessary to wait, was wont to restrain herself. Her hands, like little darter fish, could be held for only a short time before they jumped for the prize. More quickly than most children, she seemed to "forget" what she had been told.

Fortunately, there were signs that Jennifer could develop emotionally and socially. She achieved reasonable daytime toilet habits but still had problems at night. One morning before Rainelle and I separated, I awakened and found Jennifer asleep on her bed, without sheets, blankets, or pillows. She was also stark naked. I couldn't imagine what had happened. Later in the day I went to open the linen closet and was met with an overpowering stench. During the night, she had soiled her bed; rather than face disgruntled parents in the morning, she had stuffed the evidence in the closet.

Oh well, two steps forward, one step back.

A few months later Jennifer was doing well getting to the bathroom on time, but she was still having problems with the functions of toilet paper. I often tried to help her and to praise her when she was finished. One day I went to stand by the bathroom door to supervise Jennifer. Indignantly, she got up and, with her jeans only partly pulled up, stumbled over to push me out of the bathroom. Then she closed the door.

I was never so happy to have a door shut in my face.

In any event, I was sure that Jennifer didn't understand much until I found a drawing she did sometime after Christmas of 1976, when she was seven (facing page). It doesn't take a child psychologist to understand that none of these three people has ears, and that the little one isn't very happy.

108

Family portrait (1976)

The reports from Jennifer's school were encouraging. She was placed in a special education classroom with several children who had multiple handicaps in addition to deafness. One little girl had been oxygen-deprived at birth and was severely retarded. The other children had varying degrees of cerebral palsy and deafness, but they functioned at a high level. Jennifer was assigned a bed in the infirmary so her sleep habits wouldn't disturb the other children. Every night she was taken from the dormitory and across the yard to the infirmary. She was still not capable of going by herself because, being easily distracted, she might stop and play with a butterfly or an interesting insect.

A few months passed. Jennifer apparently posed no insurmountable problems for the school. Rainelle and I were talking about trying to live together again. Despite our anger, we missed each other. We began looking for a house to buy, thinking that things might be better if we had more room.

In February 1977 a snowstorm and other obligations prevented us from going to get Jennifer for several weeks. It was a bitterly cold afternoon when the streets were finally cleared. We decided to drive to Fulton to see Jennifer.

The heater in the car worked at full speed, but that was about two speeds shy of what was needed. Shivering after the long ride, we pulled into the parking lot in front of the infirmary. Snowdrifts sat in the space between the lot and buildings like frozen surf. Out of the corner of my eye I saw a child playing in the snow. There were no other children or adults in sight. As we got out of the car and walked toward the child, we saw that it was Jennifer.

"What in the world is going on?" I said to Rainelle, who rushed to pick Jennifer up.

"She could freeze out here!" Rainelle said. "My God, what if she had wandered away?"

Jennifer was not mature enough to come in out of the rain or snow. She wouldn't know she was in trouble until it was too late. My initial fear gave way to anger. I stormed into the dormitory to find out why Jennifer had been let loose in the snow with no supervision. The dorm mother apologized profusely and assured us it would not happen again. She said that Jennifer had just slipped away from them. But it was hard to be reassured. This, the only unexpected visit we'd ever made, revealed a serious problem. What happened the rest of the time?

After so many experiences like this in other times and other places, it was difficult for us to trust anyone.

There was an announcement in the paper about a noncredit sign language course. Rainelle and I knew that Jennifer would have to rely on signs and that we would have to learn the language. So we enrolled.

There is much misunderstanding about sign language. Actually there are several different methods, including fingerspelling and an English-to-sign-language translation which allows one to "speak" in English through signs. But the real means of communication by the deaf is an actual language—American Sign Language, or ASL—with unique idioms, syntax, and phrasing. Consequently, learning to sign is every bit as complex as learning to speak French or German or Spanish. The deaf are culturally influenced by their language also. As English is a good language for technical communication, sign is an excellent medium for conveying emotions.

There was much to learn.

The sign class met once a week for sixteen weeks. Our classmates included a black minister and his wife who wanted to try to communicate with deaf people in their parish. Several people had deaf children or relatives. One man had just lost his hearing and wanted a way to communicate again, but he soon dropped the class out of frustration. He had difficulty following what went on in class when everyone talked about how to sign.

One woman in the class said that she worked in the deaf classroom in the public school and had a deaf son in college. She wanted to brush up on her signs. I assumed she was a teacher's aide because her signing skills were not especially good, even by my unsophisticated standards. For example, she knew only one sign for *rest room* even though deaf signers use variations similar to English for *toilet* and *bathroom*. But that was not the time or place to quibble about the decline of standards in public education.

Before and after class, Rainelle and I looked at houses. Rainelle continued her second semester of law school, and I worked and attended graduate school. Jennifer would be home in a month or two for the summer. Then we could try to be a family again.

After months of searching, we finally found a house we liked and could afford. We were excited the night we signed the contract. Rainelle visualized where every piece of furniture would sit, where every plant would hang. We talked about how much easier Jennifer would be to manage with the fenced-in yard and large house in which to play.

After nearly eight years of living in travel trailers and apartments, we finally had our own home.

CHAPTER **8**

When Jennifer came home for the summer, she seemed so much more mature. She was using sign language expressively. She acted calmer, as if the tension in her body was being released through her hands. And oh, how tall she was getting! She was like a rosebush climbing a trellis—not much girth but plenty of height.

Rainelle and I were busy with work and school, but we both knew we would soon have to talk about where Jennifer would go to school next year. We began to feel each other out.

"That drive to Fulton is just awful," Rainelle said.

"Yeah, but that's where her school is," I replied, wishing that this conversation didn't have to happen.

"And that school just isn't what Jennifer needs," said Rainelle. "She's in class with a bunch of retarded kids. And you remember that day we went down to see her and found her in the snow. They just don't watch the children like they should."

"Rainelle, those things happen. Jennifer did survive the year, after all, so it can't be that bad."

"Well, she needs to have full-time parents."

Here we go again, I thought. "You mean you want Jennifer to live at home next year and go to school."

"Yes, I do," Rainelle said. "The school district should provide a class for her with other deaf kids. I know there is one here somewhere that will work."

"But, Rainelle, we've already agreed on this. Yes, it would be nice for Jennifer to live at home, but making arrangements for all of us to get to school and work and for babysitters is like a Chinese fire drill. It's just so nice not to have to worry about Jennifer during the week or to have to get up with her at night. She's better about that, but she's still a problem. Besides, we also agreed that Jennifer needs a deaf environment where everyone signs."

"I know, I know, but she needs parents more. You just don't want to assume responsibility for her. You'd like to just ship her off and be done with it," Rainelle said.

"That's not true," I said, and I meant it. But I still felt guilty. I had already "shipped her off" twice.

God, would this never end?

After a minute of stony silence, I relented and said, "Okay, we'll look into it. But I don't want to."

Our first step was to get the evaluation of another child psychologist—one who could support our public school plan. This was rather like shopping for the diagnosis we wanted to hear, considering the inconsistency of previous opinions. It seemed senseless, however, to go back to people who had made obvious errors in diagnosis.

We called a psychologist who had been associated with one of Jennifer's previous schools, one in which she had done well. We asked him if he would evaluate Jennifer to see if she was ready for a "regular" deaf classroom. He agreed and set the time for the tests.

His report seemed quite convincing. We thought it would give us the leverage we needed to compel the local school district to accept Jennifer.

Psychologist's Summary, August 1977
Jennifer Harris, age 7 years, 8 months

The most thorough report and demonstration of Jennifer's capabilities occurred during her year at Sherwood Center 1975–76.

114

She was very carefully taught an extensive sign vocabulary (175–200 words), reinforced by academic instruction and programmed play and peer social sessions. A precise diagnostic evaluation of Jennifer's capabilities was hampered in past years principally because of: (1) inadequate vocabulary training, (2) focus on lipreading and vocalization without adding sign language, (3) immature behavior associated with her inability to communicate, and (4) the absence of a highly structured teaching environment.

Jennifer's performance in the diagnostic evaluation I performed with her teacher revealed that: (1) in spite of small variations in standardized testing administration, this child at minimal approaches normal intelligence, (2) her use of word substitutes in comprehension and production is excellent, (3) she can easily handle symbolic and academic materials—reading, signing, writing and computation skills, (4) performance capabilities are excellent (block design, writing, Bender), (5) her long-term memory (11–13 months) is also very good and shows the normal pattern of loss, (6) arithmetic skills are advancing rapidly now that she understands what is involved in tasks, (7) she is beginning to accelerate in her use of descriptive conversational speech in free play as well as in structured settings, (8) vocabulary expansion has been demonstrated to occur at a rapid rate, with Jennifer inventing new word combinations to describe her interaction with the environment, and (9) a recent interest and increase in social play.

Teacher reports at Sherwood additionally attest to Jennifer's learning capabilities. One of the unfortunate consequences of her earlier training reflects on our inabilities as teachers to communicate to Jennifer exactly what it is that we want her to do. I have observed this! Once Jennifer catches on to the concept that is being presented, she learns and generalizes rapidly.

Jennifer's rate of learning for language handicapped children makes it imperative for her to be transferred to a normal classroom for deaf children so that her current level of development may be capitalized upon and increased.

Our next step was to explore programs in every school district close to Kansas City, hoping to find a deaf classroom that practiced sign language. Schools that used lipreading would not be adequate for Jennifer. That

115

approach, unfortunately, was being used in several districts. In the end, the Kansas City school district was the only one with a program that looked feasible.

We enrolled Jennifer. We were able to avoid argument about her ability to handle the class based on the strength of the evaluation. We just waited until classes began to see where the cards would fall.

Before classes began we took Jennifer to her new school. We walked around the playground, peeked into windows, and generally tried to get her acclimated. We showed her the hopscotch markings and tried to get her to play. In our best (still inadequate) sign language, we explained that this was her new school. Jennifer didn't seem to care much. Rainelle was excited about Jennifer's prospects in the new setting.

The school was in a quiet, older neighborhood. I imagined children playing kickball on cool autumn mornings while the other children arrived on yellow school buses. I could see them carrying Charlie Brown lunch pails and dropping them on the asphalt to join in play before the morning bell rang.

I dreamed that Jennifer might have experiences so normal, so much like my own.

On the first day of school, Rainelle met Jennifer's teacher. It was the woman we met in the sign language course the previous winter! We knew that she helped in the school district, but we assumed she was just an aide. She certainly was not a highly trained special education teacher. We were aghast to think that Jennifer would be learning to communicate from someone who could barely babble in sign language herself.

Wanting a teacher skilled in sign language didn't seem like too much to ask, so we requested that Jennifer be transferred to another classroom. We were told there were no other classrooms. Meanwhile, other problems began to occur. Bus transportation was erratic and irregular, sometimes several hours off schedule. Supervision on the playground, we found out, sometimes did not begin

116

until long after the school bus had let the children off. A conversation with the school principal about these problems generated no response, so I attempted to pierce the school district bureaucracy to find someone interested in solving the problems.

The problem with this approach was that no one person was really responsible for anything, so no one would take definite action. I was referred to Mr. X for one problem and Mr. Y for the next; they would say see Mr. Z, who would wonder why X and Y sent me to him.

As if symbolizing the communication problems, the school district switchboard was busy for an hour at a time. When a call did go through, the staff was "out of the office" nine times out of ten. It took me an entire work week, five days, to get a person-to-person phone conversation with the man who seemed to be the one I needed to talk with most. I immediately sensed disinterest if not incompetence. He hemmed and hawed and said he'd look into the problem; he pointed out that the beginning of a school year was always busy.

Anger and frustration—accumulated over the years and exacerbated by the present situation—gripped me.

Negotiations began with the school district about how to make their program suitable for Jennifer. Eventually the discussions turned to what alternative placements were available. It became rather emotional. I couldn't control my anger. The school district was legally responsible for providing an education for my child, but their program was inadequate and unsafe in my opinion. Informal communication with the teacher and supervisors failed; it succeeded only in making them defensive.

An administrator to whom I had expressed my doubts about the competence of Jennifer's teacher relayed my thoughts to the teacher. The teacher responded by verbally attacking Rainelle one afternoon when she was picking up Jennifer.

That was the last straw. Jennifer was withdrawn from school, and I wrote a letter to the district.

117

Dear Mr. Williams:

After the events of this past week regarding our daughter, Jennifer Harris, I thought it would be best to further clarify the situation in writing to help direct future action. We received a copy of our attorney's letter to you and assume you will have his letter by the time this letter arrives. Apparently you had a discussion with Ms. Smith, Jennifer's teacher, after you and I talked over the phone. The following day when my wife took Jennifer to school, Ms. Smith acted in such a manner that Jennifer was taken home from school, where she will remain until this entire matter is resolved. At this point, I think it would be best to put our communication in writing to avoid confusion and misunderstanding.

To summarize, when the teacher's assignment was given, my wife and I recalled that Ms. Smith had been a participant in a Communiversity sign language course with us. We remembered that Ms. Smith had some difficulty with signs that a teacher of the deaf probably shouldn't have. Recognizing that there are different approaches to working with the deaf which might not require fluency in sign, I nevertheless believe that Jennifer's teacher should be highly skilled in sign. Jennifer is totally deaf and has not responded to oral methods. Ms. Smith may work well with other deaf children, but she herself has expressed doubts to me regarding her ability to work with Jennifer. We expressed this concern to your office as the school year started.

Furthermore, the bus service has been so irregular that we have been unable to depend on it, in fact, frightened to do so. It shows up at our house somewhere between eight and ten o'clock. It arrived to leave Jennifer off once before school was officially out. I noticed once on a school brochure that playground supervision was not provided before 8:30 a.m. When I asked what would happen if the bus arrived before the supervisor, I was told that that "probably" wouldn't happen. One time Jennifer was sent home by cab when explicit instructions were given that she would be picked up at school. The cab deposited Jennifer at the neighbor's, who happened to be home. For other children, these things might work out OK, but Jennifer does not understand some things and will wander off if permitted. The dangers are obvious. I also understand that Jennifer was once allowed to get out of the playground area and cross the street before supervisors noticed her.

As a result of unsuccessful conversations with the representatives of the school, I retained an attorney to let you know the situation was serious and would not wait lengthy deliberation. Before school began, a private psychologist was hired to evaluate Jennifer; you have that report. In essence, it says that Jennifer is deaf but of normal intelligence and can learn in a properly structured environment. In our phone conversation, you referred to Jennifer as "hypersensitive." Ms. Smith has called her multihandicapped. Whatever your opinion or label, the fact is that Jennifer can learn. Documentation of Jennifer's progress at the Sherwood Center and last year at the Missouri School for the Deaf has, I believe, been provided.

My wife and I want Jennifer to live at home with us and to attend a classroom where enough individual attention and structure can be provided by an instructor competent in signs, though not necessarily at an extremely advanced interpreter level. Teachers with behavior modification skills who are willing to use those skills in the classroom have provided such instruction in the past for Jennifer. With funding from the school district to pay for tutoring, I believe good instruction can be arranged again by some of Jennifer's previous teachers. At this point we would like your recommendation.

In part, because of the behavior of Ms. Smith toward my wife on the day previously mentioned, I believe that Ms. Smith is prejudiced against Jennifer to such an extent that Jennifer's progress would be hindered if she returned to that classroom. I previously recommended that a qualified aide in the classroom might solve most of the problems. Ms. Smith and I discussed the need for an aide, but she apparently has changed her mind. In any event, Jennifer will not be returned to that classroom now.

I would appreciate a detailed, written response from the school district. I don't believe a hearing is necessary as the situation has been described and discussed orally and

now in writing. However, should you think it necessary, I
will appear.

Sincerely,
George A. Harris

The administrator studiously avoided putting anything in writing. He wanted to arrange an informal
meeting to discuss our problems. I assured him of my
intention to pursue the matter through legal channels,
having become familiar with federal law which mandates
appropriate, individualized education programs for handicapped children in public schools.

Though I was angry at the school district, I was also
angry at Rainelle. If she had just let Jennifer stay at the
school for the deaf, all this trouble would never be
happening. Now, it seemed, I was left with the responsibility for fighting the battles and straightening out the mess.

If the school district couldn't remedy the current
situation, we were prepared to ask it to pay the costs of
private school. Before the meeting, Rainelle and I called
one of Jennifer's old schools in Kansas City to arrange for
her to attend there. It was the Operation Discovery
private elementary school that combined classes of normal and handicapped children. The problem with the
school was that the teachers didn't know sign language. I
proposed to hire an interpreter to go into the school to
tutor Jennifer. The school, however, eagerly agreed to
hire the interpreter on a part-time basis with part of the
tuition the state would eventually pay. The staff liked
Jennifer and seemed willing to do whatever they could to
help her.

The day arrived to meet with the school administrator.
Loaded for bear, I went to the meeting, accompanied by
my attorney, one of Jennifer's former teachers, and the
child psychologist who had examined Jennifer. Both the
former teacher and the psychologist were prepared to
argue that Jennifer should be able to function effectively

in any adequate deaf classroom. Because there were problems with her assignment in the Kansas City school district, this called into question the adequacy of the district's deaf education program.

The meeting was held in the central office of the school district. It took several minutes for the security guard at the main door to find out if the person we said we wanted to see really worked there. Eventually he located a room number and allowed us to enter. After a few minutes, two men entered the room. Both men were administrators in the district's special education program.

After introductions, my attorney began the meeting.

"Mr. and Mrs. Harris are concerned about the quality of education being provided their daughter here. It is our position that the school district is obligated to provide adequate supervision and instruction for all students. There have been many other problems such as bus service that present a danger to Jennifer. These problems are unacceptable, and we are here to determine how the district will arrange for Jennifer's education."

One of the administrators sat silently, leaning back in his chair, while the other, Mr. Williams, spoke.

"Now, Mr. and Mrs. Harris have made some very serious accusations about the competency of one of our teachers, a woman with much experience and a master's degree in education."

"That's beside the point," I interrupted. "First, we don't know if her degree is in special education. I assume you'll provide evidence of that. Second, she herself admits she is not trained in manual communication other than through her own experiences, and she has also said she doesn't know how to work with a child like Jennifer who has no speech at all."

"Mr. Harris, your child does present some special problems beyond deafness. She is multiply handicapped, and the class she was in is not for those children," Mr. Williams said.

I was furious.

121

"Listen. What evidence do you have to call her that?" I asked. "The reports in front of you, and these two people with me, who have taught and evaluated Jennifer, say that a competent and properly trained teacher of the deaf should be able to work with Jennifer. If you don't have the facilities to do that, just say so."

"Mr. Harris, we have a first-rate special education program . . ."

"But you're saying Jennifer is too weird to fit in. So what do you propose to do besides sending her back to Fulton, which her mother and I have said is unacceptable."

"Well, we'd like to have your input on that. Of course, we'd like for Jennifer to be in good hands."

I had come to this meeting with no expectations of the school district changing its staff or structure to accommodate Jennifer. I didn't even expect that they would come up with any proposals or recommendations. That would be left up to us.

The school district, after all, had been unwilling to hire the right kind of teachers and assistants in the first place. The reality was that Jennifer's teacher had been teaching since there were only twenty known chemical elements. She had no training in modern deaf education, and everybody in the room knew it. But the administrators couldn't get rid of her if they wanted to. She had seniority. Meanwhile, my daughter was left out.

"Okay," I said. "Here's our proposal. We suggest that you pay for Jennifer to attend private school."

I handed out a letter with my written recommendation, naming the school, the teachers, and the sign language tutor who had already begun to work with Jennifer.

The administrators were stuck. They had already said that Jennifer didn't fit into their program because she was multihandicapped. They didn't have any other suggestions, so they had to take mine.

Naturally, no decision could be made final until a

thousand other bureaucrats had time to consider the recommendations. I asked what Jennifer should do until official approval was given. No one had any suggestions. So I said that Jennifer would be enrolled and that we would expect tuition to be paid retroactive to the date of enrollment. (Official approval came two months later.)

All of my frustration was not yet vented, though. I found this out when, after the meeting, the silent administrator approached me.

"You know," he said, "if you'd only work with us, we'd be able to avoid meetings like this."

I turned toward him, glaring in old but freshly renewed anger.

"I can't believe you said that. I make phone calls that are never returned, write letters that are never answered, and my wife takes the abuse of an inadequate teacher. My recommendations for classroom changes and additional aides are ignored. You risk the very life of my child with your lousy, poorly managed bus service and supervision, and you want me to be reasonable!"

"George, George," my attorney said as he hustled me out the door. "We got what we needed. Let's leave it, okay?"

As we drove home I thought that in another life, another world, another plane of existence, maybe I wouldn't be so mean-spirited. Maybe I would be more forgiving. But in this world, today, I retained a slow burning rage toward people more concerned with saving face than a child's life.

Later in the evening, when the flame was a memory and not a sensation, I joked with myself in my best Bogart impression of an ex-con talking out of the side of his mouth: "All right, all right, no more Mr. Nice Guy." Even with the joking, though, I knew a change had happened. My emotional wounds were not healed so much as cauterized. A more calculating callousness was beginning to emerge. It receded only when I watched Jennifer play.

Perhaps someday, Jennifer, you'll be able to read this, my thoughts on your eighth birthday. You don't understand more than just a few basic signs now, so I can't adequately tell you what is in my heart. Maybe someday, though. Until then, I have only this to express myself.

I referred to you as "my baby" the other day while talking to a friend. He laughed and said you weren't a baby anymore, but it's hard not to think of you as my baby. In many ways you've grown up, though in many ways you haven't. That's what makes it all so confusing. You still can't play outside by yourself or tie your shoes, but you go to school and take your lunch with you, and you're about to lose your first tooth.

It's quite a tooth, too. We've pushed and pulled, tugged and tickled that tooth. It should be out and under your pillow before long. Like most things in your life, it hasn't come easily. Soon though, the tooth fairy can trade a comic book for your tooth—money might not mean anything to you where the Incredible Hulk would.

Your mother and I were just now talking about the future. Both of us know that you might never be independent of us, that you might never be able to live outside a sheltered setting of some kind. Compared to our feelings of a couple of years ago, these are optimistic and satisfying thoughts. Still, it would be a lie to say I'm not saddened by the prospect of your living so dependent on others. Myself, I'm already very weary of responsibility. For so many reasons, some selfish, I hope things continue to look bright for your future.

I bought you "Stretch Monster" for your birthday because you acted so excited when it was advertised on TV. Your mother bought you a pretty baby doll, but Stretch Monster, the green stretchable hunk of plastic with a gruesome face, won the popularity contest hands down. What a crazy world, when an eight year old would rather tuck in a monster than a doll baby. The written instructions with Stretch Monster said that he was really a sweet monster except when angry and that Stretch Armstrong (his stretchable plastic adversary) makes him very, very angry. Maybe I'm lucky that you can't read, or Stretch Armstrong would need to be on your Christmas list. It's been fun seeing you get pleasure from that silly toy. You mime the monster to describe what happens when you pull on its arms. If you could talk, you probably wouldn't be such a good actress . . . or nearly as funny.

I guess there's a strong chance you'll realize, someday, that you are different from other kids. When that happens, maybe I'll be able to answer your questions so you'll understand and not be bitter about it. I hope so. You've come a long way in eight years; I'm very proud of you every time you learn to sign a new word or figure out a new way to play with and tease me, even without words. I'm proud of how much your mother and I have been able to help you, too, though it never seems to be enough. Maybe you'll never appreciate that help—maybe you'll think we should have done more. Then again, maybe you'll wish we had done more but be satisfied that we've done what we could. That would be best of all.

Just six months ago your mother and I went to see you in your first school play. We couldn't imagine that they'd be able to teach you an actual part in the play (which turned out to be the *Wizard of Oz*), and they hadn't. But seeing Dorothy and the Lion speaking in signs was no match for watching you dance in a warm-up to the play, "The Spring Dance." I held my breath when you took the stage, gasped when they let go of your hands (I was afraid you'd run), and marveled when you did your pirouettes, *almost* in unison with the other dancers. You kept sneaking glances out to the audience, as if to make sure we were still there watching your wonderful performance. When you returned to your seat with your class three rows in front of us, you kept turning around, and we kept signing "good girl, proud of you." There's no way to be sure what a little girl like you really feels, but you seemed quite proud of yourself and happy to have pleased us.

I write this now because two years ago I never dreamed you'd be able to do what you did. And between the Spring Dance and now, your eighth birthday, you've come even further, and it feels so good to have hope for you.

Whatever the future brings, my love, I hope it holds moments like now, for all of us. Happy Birthday.

CHAPTER 9

As I reflect on my life with Jennifer and Rainelle, I see lots of things I could have done differently if only I'd known how. But then I'm sure I'll say the same thing again in a few years about what I'm doing now. My only real regrets result from not doing my best with the knowledge and skill I have at the time. In the present, without benefit of hindsight, I think most parents with handicapped children are doing their best. That doesn't mean they're doing everything perfectly, but rather that their intentions are good. Professional people trying to help families need to understand this.

Jennifer is not the only one who is growing. I have grown with her. I have learned about things beyond my immediate predicament.

For example, I recognize that much of my anger at the administrators in the school district in Kansas City was harbored from so many earlier experiences and hurts. They too were just individuals in a huge bureaucracy that no one created. Recognizing this drains off some of my anger but not my determination to prevent Jennifer from suffering because of inadequate services.

I've also gained new understanding of my relationship

with Rainelle. At the very beginning of our marriage I was not involved enough with either Rainelle or Jennifer. Rainelle and Jennifer were bonded as mothers and children tend to be. I was like many fathers in my detachment from the family. When I began to show more concern for Jennifer by participating in the decision making about her education, the differences between Rainelle and me began to emerge.

I see much more clearly now that Rainelle and I established roles that we played, unsatisfying as they were. I played the responsible, rational father, and Rainelle played the emotional mother. Like magnets, we either clung together or, if a certain position was achieved, we repelled each other with an equal, invisible force. I was unable to show Rainelle my doubts, my weaknesses. Rainelle could not reveal her strengths.

Jennifer was only the issue around which these roles revolved. Other couples may use a different issue. Any stress will do. Then couples can become like the North and South Poles.

Rainelle and I were faced with numerous real stresses. We were too busy, too poor, too young, and we had a daughter with too many problems. These were real problems, but they weren't handled as they might have been by someone else. I certainly never was one to share my intimate thoughts with Rainelle. I never showed her my diary, and as late as 1978 Rainelle showed surprise when I spoke of my love for our daughter. With communication like that, marital problems are not unexpected.

I felt such an intense isolation. I thought that no one, not even Rainelle, could help. Doctors, audiologists, teachers, friends, and even my wife could not be trusted to understand. The burden, the responsibility was mine, and I was resentful. Ever so gradually, the process of sharing my feelings with others began to help me feel less alone.

It was irrational, I know, but I even resented Rainelle for the stress I felt during the encounter with the school district in Kansas City. I was angry because Rainelle couldn't accept the fact that schools were going to be imperfect. With work, school, and Jennifer, I felt drained, parched like a reservoir during a drought. I felt my soul becoming hardened and cracked like sun-baked mud.

But I wanted more. No, I ached for more. I wanted a marriage where I felt safe to share my weaknesses, my guilt over Jennifer, my feelings of being inadequate, of being unable to provide a decent living. I wanted someone who could share secret communications with me at a party with a wink or a nod, but I didn't know how to ask for it from Rainelle. Clearly, something was wrong. I just didn't know what.

Eventually I recognized that our differences were not just over Jennifer. They went much deeper. For example, when I first wanted to institutionalize Jennifer, I may really have been forcing Rainelle to choose between Jennifer and me. I felt that Rainelle loved Jennifer at my expense, and I wanted to test the hunch.

Perhaps the ultimate piece of hindsight, and the ultimate in oversimplification, is to say that our problems began with our reasons for getting married. The marriage was not freely chosen, and all the problems that followed were magnified by that fact. One does not force such choices without costs. I certainly shared the responsibility for Jennifer, but I was too young and immature to choose marriage freely and, deep inside, I doubted that Rainelle freely chose me. To expect love to flourish under such conditions is like looking for gold in the streets. All I really knew then was that I didn't feel loved and that I was angry and resentful. No doubt Rainelle also felt rejected. From the beginning it was so much more natural for each of us to show personal anger than to share common hurt.

As time passed, I felt more tenderness for Jennifer, but I felt less and less for Rainelle. We spent so little time together. Work and school consumed most of our time and energy, leaving little time for each other. Then again, perhaps work and school became our excuses for avoiding time together. The less time we were together, the less we seemed to want to try to make time. We didn't show affection to one another.

It is hard to have one's priorities in order under such circumstances and at such an early age.

One day in conversation a friend compared marriage to gardening. She said both must be cultivated or else the weeds take over and the plants cannot bear fruit. Some gardens are so far gone from neglect that they must be tilled and started anew.

When I was a boy, my grandfather, a farmer, allowed me to start a garden near his house. I planted a row of lettuce, a row of corn, a row of this and that. I watered the garden and tilled it. I watched the heads of lettuce leaf out and the corn grow tall.

Sweet corn on the cob was always my favorite. As the summer passed, I anticipated feasting on the result of my labor.

One day I thought the corn looked ready. The tassles were brown and the ears big. Grandpa told me to get a few ears and open them to see how they looked.

"Grandpa," I said. "There's something wrong. The corn doesn't have enough kernels. It's all cob."

"That's right," he said. "You only planted one row. Corn needs at least two rows or it won't cross-pollinate."

"But Grandpa," I said, "why didn't you tell me when I started the garden? I spent the whole summer working on the garden, and now there's no corn."

He paused, looked at me and said, "I figured you'd remember it better this way."

So gardens and marriages not only have to be cultivated, they have to be planted right in the first place.

Rainelle and I separated, but we decided not to divorce yet. We vowed to try our utmost to keep our feelings about each other from interfering with Jennifer. I do not know how much Jennifer really understood what was happening. I am equally unsure to what extent the problems between Rainelle and me affected her behavior.

I always have a hard time imagining how parents of severely handicapped children can avoid having extra stress put on their marriages. But if these children make marriage more stressful, they also make separation and divorce more difficult because of guilt and concern for the child's day-to-day welfare. I wondered whether Rainelle or I could manage Jennifer alone. I knew I wasn't ready for the total responsibility. The decision to separate was difficult. There were no rule books to use to judge the correctness of the decision.

Although Jennifer added much stress to the marital relationship, these tensions were not really the main issues in the marriage. If Rainelle and I had loved each other more maturely, we would have found ways to stay together despite Jennifer's problems. It is even possible that we could have grown closer by working together to overcome the obstacles in the way of Jennifer's development. Instead, we sometimes used the difficulties she presented as an excuse for our own dissatisfaction. It was easy to blame our tenseness with each other on the many disappointments we faced with Jennifer and with the institutions that seemed to care so much less for Jennifer than we did.

How does one explain attitudes formed by hundreds of incidents and thoughts? Jennifer. So unpredictable, so hard to explain. When she was six years old, she became fascinated with belly buttons and, for some reason, proceeded to check everyone's. With lightning speed she yanked my shirt out of my pants and looked for my belly button. Man or woman, stranger or friend was subject to search without warning. My notes do not record the last time Jennifer checked a belly button, but I think it was about 1978. The ritual disappeared as inexplicably as it had arrived.

I also do not precisely remember the last time Jennifer

wore her most fascinating clothes combination. She delighted in wearing nothing but socks pulled over her hands and a pair of panties on her head. Placed so her ponytail stuck out through the leg openings, the panties looked like a special surgical headdress for a tiny lady surgeon. She paraded through the house in this apparel, oblivious to the laughter. She seemed so different from her early years.

As Jennifer's language skills grew in the spring of 1978, she struggled to talk about things around her, much as I struggled to talk about feelings in myself. How can I explain the pleasure of watching her search her memory for a sign she wanted to make? If she came to something she couldn't label, she paused, looked upward, and put her finger on her bottom lip in a look of perplexity.

Sometimes, I thought, I love her more than Aunt Jemima loves pancakes.

Then there was Jennifer's display of almost preternatural sensitivity in certain circumstances. She displayed this whenever I doubted her ability to notice and understand what was happening around her. One evening I decided to take her to a park where the *Wizard of Oz* was to be performed in an open arena. We took a blanket and arrived early to get a good spot. The evening was beautiful, warm and balmy, and Jennifer was in a good mood. As we spread out the blanket, Jennifer signed, "Rain, rain."

I ignored her because the sky looked beautiful. But she persisted. "Rain, rain," she signed again.

"No rain, look," I signed, pointing to the sky. Jennifer, however, was unconvinced.

"Rain," she signed again.

Changing the subject, I diverted her attention to the stage and to the crowd that was gathering.

Ten minutes passed. Night was closing in, but the sky did seem to be getting dark awfully fast.

"Rain," Jennifer signed.

I was tired of that line by then.

The orchestra began tuning up; the show was about to begin. A strong wind began to lift the corners of our blanket. I noticed the absence of stars in the sky. The audience hushed as the stage lights were turned on and the orchestra roared into the first bars of "Over the Rainbow."

At that precise moment, a clap of thunder pealed over the park; a few drops of rain, then a cascade of water, poured over the crowd.

"Hey, great effects," one wiseacre yelled.

Jennifer, laughing excitedly as we raced for cover, signed, "Rain, Father, rain."

I vowed never to ignore her again. The incident made me wonder just how much she understood about the problems between her mother and me.

Jennifer stayed primarily with Rainelle, but there were many times when she needed me to watch Jennifer. So it was not a typical separation, if such a thing even exists. Frequently the three of us got together to do things. One weekend we took Jennifer to a carnival. She loved the rides and, of course, the cotton candy, and we indulged her considerably. It was fun to watch her have fun.

The carnival workers were stereotypical Runyanesque characters—grimy, unshaven, shady-looking. But Jennifer couldn't have cared less about the unsophisticated ambiance as long as she was plied with cotton candy.

We were walking along, signing and laughing, when Jennifer motioned that she wanted to ride the Ferris wheel. We walked up to the operator. He looked like a steamship stowaway, and I felt like I should put my hand over my wallet. I handed him the ticket, but he wouldn't take it.

"I noticed your little girl," he said. "I been around lots of them little kids doing volunteer work and all. It's real expensive raising them little devils, I know, so you all just save your ticket for the next ride. That way she can have an extra ride."

I thanked him as graciously as I could, given my astonishment. Then I stood back to watch Jennifer be treated to what must have been the longest ride in carnival history.

As the wheel spun around, I thought how hard it was to tell the good guys from the bad guys. If I was not seeing much good in people, maybe I was looking in the wrong places.

Rainelle and I were managing to get along separately. She was struggling in law school. I, about to finish my Ph.D., received an offer to teach at a small university in Topeka, Kansas, sixty miles from Kansas City. When we learned that Jennifer would be able to go to the Kansas State School for the Deaf in Olathe if I became a resident of Kansas, I took the job.

With this arrangement Jennifer could stay in the dormitory at the school, which was about thirty minutes away from Rainelle and ninety minutes from me. Rainelle was satisfied with Jennifer's living there, because she knew that school arrangements in Kansas City were not really adequate. So Jennifer was enrolled in the school and was placed in a classroom with two other multi-handicapped deaf girls.

Jennifer's new teacher, Mrs. Busch, was a distinct improvement over some of her earlier teachers. Mrs. Busch was proficient at sign language. She was also meticulous about her own and Jennifer's hygiene. But most important, she seemed to care about Jennifer as a person.

One of the first things she tried to teach Jennifer was how to express and label feelings. For example, if Jennifer felt angry, Mrs. Busch tried to teach her how to sign "I am angry" rather than to throw a fit.

Mrs. Busch also worked with Jennifer to prepare her for visits to the doctor and dentist. Before Jennifer's trip to the dentist, she got the three girls in the class to play-act the experience. They sat in chairs and looked into each other's mouths so that the real thing wouldn't be so scary.

The rehearsal was effective; Jennifer's visit to the dentist went well. A weekend or so after the visit, Jennifer walked over to me as I lay on the couch. She propped open my jaw and began examining my teeth with the aid of a flashlight. I was just glad there were no loose needles around for her to use for added realism.

It was certainly nice not to have to worry about Jennifer's education. And Rainelle, Jennifer, and I got together just often enough that it was pleasant to see each other. As the end of Jennifer's first semester neared, I felt an uncharacteristic stability to our lives.

[Diary, December 1978]

I don't dream about Jennifer often, or anyone I know well for that matter. Although it's possible my friends and family appear symbolically, I don't make the connection if they do. So, when Jennifer does show up in my nightly meanderings, it seems important to pay close attention. I remember one such dream four years ago.

In 1974, life was not particularly enjoyable. Jennifer seemed to drain all available emotional, mental, and financial resources, and I resented it. One night that year I dreamed that Jennifer was seated at my place at the dinner table, and there were no other chairs. No one else at the food-laden table seemed to notice or care that there was no room for me. What an ogre I would have seemed if I had made Jennifer give me my place back. I stood there, feeling rather lonesome and rejected, looking down at a meal I had provided but couldn't share.

Jennifer is now nine. Although she has no concept of what a year is, she is for the first time anticipating Christmas. She thumbs through Christmas catalogs, gesturing animatedly at dolls and other toys. TV commercials result

134

in a slap to daddy's knees, just to be sure he's paying attention. Bathroom towels are wrapped around old toys, and last year's ribbons and bows decorate the packages. She's still not a normal child, but Jennifer can be great fun to be around. Times and feelings change.

Jennifer has developed a love of money. It is typical of her slow social development that, not understanding the concept of an amount of money, she prefers pennies to nickels, dimes, or quarters. Penny gumball machines are favorite targets for her attention. Smiling, she will approach total strangers and solicit money, holding out her hand, palm up. Sometimes they oblige, not out of pity, but as if it is an honor to give this little girl money. Jennifer's housemother at school chuckles at how Jennifer mischievously demands pennies for kisses. In some ways, so immature, in others, surprisingly sophisticated. Maybe with enough mischievousness, she stands a good chance of surviving in the world.

Over the years, much of Jennifer's behavior has been unpleasant. But when she was nine I had softer memories of some of that unpleasantness. She had several rather strange behaviors that caused both her and me considerable consternation. She always loved stuffed animals, for example, but she used to delight in turning on the kitchen range and throwing her Teddy Bear on the burner. Quickly after the act, she would run out of the kitchen shrieking. After the fire was doused, she never seemed to understand why the bear was not available for cuddling. The look of heartbreak on her face when I threw her bear in the trash was a sight to see.

Several times Rainelle and I bought an identical replacement bear only to have it put on the pyre. Apparently Jennifer enjoyed the excitement of the moment more than the long-range, albeit less intense, satisfactions of moderate use of her toy. Her habit resembled the behavior of many other people, such as alcoholics; it was a pattern not easy to stop.

The origin of this behavior may have been in the back seat of a car on hot summer days. While the family was riding down the road, Jennifer delighted in throwing her plastic bottle out the side window, then looking out the back window to watch the bottle bounce off the pavement and disappear as the car moved away.

Invariably she would do this, then, as if realizing the import of her act, would begin to wail in grief as she motioned for me to turn the car around to retrieve her possession. Eventually, any loose object became fair game. Anything from comic books to tennis balls was in mortal danger of propulsion from the back seat of the car.

Hard-nosed child psychologists might advise parents not to try to retrieve objects treated in this manner, in order to teach children that their actions have real consequences. That's all well and good until kiddy throws out a ten dollar toy—or daddy's tennis racket.

I decided it was cheaper and easier to buy a car with air conditioning so I could roll up the windows. I wanted air conditioning anyway, and I hoped Jennifer would just grow out of her problem.

Punishment was not only distasteful to me but I didn't figure it would work. What could be more punishing than to lose or break one's favorite possession? When I did retrieve valuable objects, I put them in the trunk for a few days so she couldn't play with them. But it was very difficult to be consistent with Jennifer. When we left the house to get in the car, she would go stand in back by the trunk, resisting getting into the car until I got her toy.

Jennifer did not restrict her problem behavior to kitchens and cars. Bathrooms were excellent places for exciting action once the toilet's flushing mechanism was discovered. Some of Jennifer's favorite playthings were small objects that fit in the palm of her hand or over the tips of her fingers, such as play shoes for small dolls. No one can imagine how many of these have been flushed down the toilet in Jennifer's career.

136

One incident in particular typified Jennifer's impulsive, live-for-the-thrill-of-the-moment behavior. I was clothes shopping with Jennifer when she found a tiny stuffed bear on the floor of the store. She clutched at it as though it were a long lost friend, and she wouldn't relinquish it.

Normally, I didn't give in to her demands in a store, no matter how much she protested. But this time my heart wanted to make her happy. It was such a small thing anyway. So I bought it for her. At the cash register, the clerk didn't know the cost, and it was almost impossible to get the bear out of Jennifer's hand long enough to check the price.

At home later that evening, Jennifer went upstairs, bear in hand as it had been all day. I heard the toilet flush. Suddenly Jennifer came racing down the stairs, a look of sheer horror on her face. She gestured wildly for me to come. I knew what had happened, but I went with her just to be sure. In the bathroom she signed that bear had "fallen" in the toilet.

All I could do was sign, "Sorry, bear is gone, sorry."

Unwilling to accept the truth, Jennifer peered into the bowl, looked up at me plaintively, and began to sob. She flushed the toilet again, hoping, I suppose, that bear could swim back. It didn't.

It took Jennifer most of the evening to recover from her loss. She went to bed a sad, but I think wiser, little girl.

As in all of life, you pay for your thrills.

By May 1979 I was sure Jennifer was through throwing things out windows. The weather was nice one spring day, so I rolled down the car windows. I told Jennifer to hold on to her yellow stuffed animal, not to throw it out. She nodded yes and held the animal tightly in her lap, as if to assure me there would be no accidents.

One mile went by, then two. I relaxed. Animal was still in Jennifer's lap.

Another mile passed. Then, out of the corner of my eye, I saw a streak of yellow fly out of the window.

Jennifer's arms had not moved more than six inches. It was as if a stray current of electricity had jolted her, forcing a sudden jerk of her arms.

Even Jennifer looked surprised.

It was the "bad" Jennifer that threw the animal; after the "good" Jennifer had regained control, she was terribly upset.

When she is good, she is very, very good, and when she is bad. . . .

I was angry, but I also felt sorry for her. Besides, the play of expressions on her face was hilarious—three emotions for the price of one.

Although Jennifer was often uninhibited, she did show concern for how she appeared to other people. By age nine she liked to be told she was pretty. She was mortified to try on clothes without a proper dressing room. She noticed babies and signed that she was a big girl now, not a baby. So when she cried or complained about not getting something she wanted, I told her she was acting like a baby. Sometimes I held her in my lap like a baby and pretended to give her a bottle. If I was lucky, she giggled in appreciation of my joke and pretended to be my baby again by sucking on my little finger.

Her sense of humor also developed in many other ways. She laughed when I play-acted animals. I played a dog that bit her leg; then a lion that shook its head and roared. She giggled when I purposefully called things by the wrong name. If I told her my name was Jennifer she corrected me and closed her eyes quickly so I couldn't argue with her in sign language. I waited for her. When she peeked at me, I quickly signed the mistake again and the game continued.

Much of Jennifer's development is reflected in her drawings. At age seven (page 109) she revealed very clearly her perception of herself at an unhappy moment. I suppose Mommy and Daddy must have looked like ogres

Pumpkin
October

Turkey
November

Santa Claus
December

Snowman
January

Valentine   Shamrock
February   March

Easter Bunny
April

Representing the months (1979)

People in motion (1979)

at this time. At age nine she showed awareness of the seasons by drawing figures representing months (page 139): a pumpkin for October, a turkey for November, etc. Also at age nine, Jennifer's drawings of people became more complete, including fingers and all facial parts. She also introduced motion, a sign of developing intelligence. One drawing (page 139) shows her people walking—not bad for a kid the doctors once called profoundly retarded.

Jennifer still had problems, though it was hard to pin them down with an abstract label; I no longer wondered why professional diagnoses were inconsistent. She still had to be told at nine years old to stop before walking into the street. One night we stopped for ice cream; on the way back to the car, parked across the street, Jennifer paused, looked both ways for cars, and continued when she saw it was safe. I was excited!

Unfortunately, she then stopped right in the middle of the street and began to eat her ice cream, oblivious to oncoming traffic.

With all of Jennifer's problems, it was so nice for her to have a teacher who cared enough to try to overcome them. A good teacher is the core of a successful school. How can you adequately express feelings of gratitude to someone who cares for your child almost as much as you do? I could relate many incidents to try to convey what such people are like. Instead I'll share a letter we received from Jennifer's teacher, updating us on progress that year. Love and humor flowed off the page.

February 10, 1979

Dear Mr. and Mrs. Harris:

Needless to say, Jennifer is very excited about Valentines. We've been cutting out hearts and learning to sing Valentine songs.

Today at lunch we had lemon pie for dessert. I asked Jennifer if she wanted her pie. She said—"no, throw up sick infirmary eat pie." Well, was I pleased to get that much of an answer. I let her know how excited I was and I took the pie.

The children saw a movie after lunch about the "Turtle and the Rabbit." This afternoon she drew a picture from the movie and told me—"Movie turtle run fast slow." I asked her "Who won?" She told me "turtle won."

Jennifer is really using language now, and I'm so excited for her.

Sincerely,
Mrs. Busch

CHAPTER 10

During the summer of 1979 Jennifer was out of school, Rainelle was in school, and I was teaching part-time during the summer session. So Jennifer stayed at my place in Topeka much of the summer. I took her to work with me while I did paperwork. As long as she had soda pop she stayed fairly quiet for short periods of time. I found an art class for children at the university, and Jennifer attended that. It was nice to have her with me.

Every morning Jennifer and I went to the swimming pool. Jennifer was afraid of the water. She would do no more than dangle her feet while sitting on the rim of the pool. Nonetheless, I always put her swimsuit and life jacket on her just in case she changed her mind. One of my fondest memories is a vision of Jennifer wearing a pert little pair of red sunglasses, her slinky swimsuit, and a life jacket that would float Kate Smith.

One day after I swam my laps, I got out of the pool, dried off, and Jennifer and I headed for the car. She spotted a sign with the pool rules on it. She wanted me to read it to her. I began, making up signs or pantomiming when I didn't know the exact sign.

"No running," I began.

"No diving off shallow end."

"No glass bottles," I continued as Jennifer watched attentively.

"No children without parents."

Finally, "No loud radios."

Jennifer signed all the rules again. Then she paused and I could almost see the light bulb in her little head come on as she signed, "No, no, no, all wrong." For a little "retarded" kid, she generalized pretty well.

That same summer Jennifer and I attended a workshop for families with deaf children sponsored by Gallaudet, the college for the deaf in Washington, D.C. The workshop was at a community college in Johnson County, Kansas, and was attended by about a dozen families. While I took classes in sign language, Jennifer participated in activities with the other children, one of whom she remembered from the Missouri School for the Deaf. He was a boy who had been adopted by two middle-aged people, both of whom I met at the workshop. I wondered what had led them to adopt him, but I never asked.

The workshop families all stayed in the same dormitory for two weeks. It was interesting to see other families interact. Some of the parents insisted that their children eventually would be oral. Others were quite proud of their children's signing skills.

As I watched some of the other children's behavior problems, including the siblings who could hear, Jennifer seemed less and less unusual. In fact, I far preferred her to any other kid. Naturally.

The staff was also interesting to observe. One evening a group of parents and a counselor, Jerry, gathered in a lounge to talk. The children were all in bed. As the hour grew late everyone became rather silly and began to tell stories.

Things were getting pretty raucous when Jerry, a budding family therapist who'd never been married, suddenly looked concerned.

"Gosh, maybe we shouldn't be so loud; we'll wake the kids," he said.

A whole roomful of parents paused, looked at one another, then broke into screams of laughter.

"Jerry, most of the kids are deaf," someone finally explained, "and the rest would already be out here if the noise bothered them."

What every parent there realized without having to say, Jerry had to have explained. But we were glad to do it, to help educate him.

Jennifer's language skills continued to improve that summer. For example, she learned the sign for *silly* and chastised her grandmother for acting that way. She also learned how to tease and be teased. I might tell Jennifer that her soda pop would taste terrible, and that she'd better let me have it. She quickly learned when I was kidding. Then she broadened her conceptual use of the word. If I told her she had to drink all of her milk, she would tell me I was just teasing; it was hard to keep a straight face and look convincing.

Jennifer also spent lots of time with her mother during the summer. Rainelle continued to work hard with Jennifer on language development. She made a set of cards with English words on them and another set with pictures of the objects represented by the words. Jennifer had to match the cards, and she learned to read many new words. Rainelle and Mrs. Busch—Jennifer's teacher at the Kansas State School for the Deaf—worked together on sign language. So Rainelle's ability to communicate manually with Jennifer also improved.

But the summer soon came to an end. It was time to trade the Kate Smith life jacket for Big Chief tablets again. Jennifer, for once in her life, had a sure place to which to return. Mrs. Busch was ready to teach Jennifer for the second year. Rainelle had some grade problems in law school. Her degree program would take a little longer to complete than she'd planned, but one more year might do the trick. My teaching job was both interesting and secure. Everything seemed to be going as smoothly as could be expected.

In fact, everything went quite well for several months. Rainelle and I still had not made any firm moves one way or the other about our marriage. I was content to let things slide for the time. I felt some tension, though, about being neither married nor divorced.

Christmas came and went. The months sped by. One weekend during a discussion with Rainelle about Jennifer, it dawned on us that Jennifer's heart hadn't been examined in several years, even though it seemed like only yesterday that the tests were done. The cardiologist at that time said Jennifer had a slight defect that might need surgery someday if it didn't correct itself.

Rainelle took Jennifer to the hospital for an examination and called me later that day. The X rays showed an enlargement of the heart, which meant the defect was causing problems and probably would require surgery. But before any final decision was made, more tests would have to be done. They would require a day or two to complete.

Those tests were no more encouraging. So we made arrangements to meet with a surgeon (my God, the surgeon!) and set a date for the operation—open heart surgery.

I couldn't believe how I had managed to cover up and to lie to myself about Jennifer's heart condition. We knew since her early years that it existed, but I never really believed anything would have to be done. I had convinced myself that the hole would close itself up, as the doctors suggested it might, or that it was so small and insignificant it would never need repair.

The lie faded as we sat talking with the surgeon. He explained how his team would put a patch over the hole and then stitch up the valve near the hole, which had sagged some over the years.

"It's a very standard operation these days," he said.

145

I saved my worst question for last.

"What are the risks, the odds?" I asked.

"Surgery always has some risks," he said. "I'd estimate that we lose between two and four percent of cases like this."

My mind froze in terror. I screamed inside about the unfairness of it all. We sat silently. I cannot remember how much time passed.

Four percent was too much risk. After all this time, to lose Jennifer now would be more than I could manage.

But the surgery had to be done. It was scheduled for midsummer so that Jennifer wouldn't miss any school.

The days, which had been passing so quickly, slowed as we waited for the day to go to the hospital. It was difficult motivating myself to do anything until the ordeal was over. I did, however, force myself into attending a two-week sign language course.

While attending the course, a friend asked if I remembered the middle-aged woman I had met the previous summer, the one who had adopted Jennifer's friend at the Missouri School for the Deaf. I was told that she committed suicide. This made me even more depressed.

Jennifer came to stay with me again when school was out, and we did various things to pass the time. I began to let Jennifer walk across the street to the park by herself. I coached her carefully on watching for cars, but each time she left the house my heart was in my throat.

My parents came to visit me for a few days. They took Jennifer to the zoo and for a ride on the miniature train. Jennifer threw her Sesame Street Big Bird out of the moving train. I reflected on how much work still needed to be done with her.

Given her uncertain future, maybe the surgery would be a merciful end to all the pain and heartbreak, I thought guiltily at times.

The stress of waiting for the surgery was awful. Finally it was Saturday and time to go to the hospital. A nurse/social worker helped us check in, explained how things would be done, and suggested how we could explain the surgery to Jennifer. Jennifer's teacher, Mrs. Busch, came to the hospital to help Rainelle and me do the explaining.

The surgery was scheduled for Monday morning. The hours passed slowly. Finally it was time for Jennifer to leave her room for the operation. Helplessly I watched the nurses roll her bed away.

My heart sank. I feared I would never see her alive again. Heart surgery seemed so awesome, and it seemed so unfair. Jennifer, with all her other problems, should not have to endure it.

The surgery lasted about three hours which, mercifully, passed quickly. Soon, the surgeon and the nurse met Rainelle and me in a waiting room and explained that everything had gone well. Jennifer would return to the intensive care unit in a few minutes. We would be allowed to see her shortly.

This wait seemed interminable. But it too passed, and we were allowed in. There she was with tubes in her nose, tubes in her veins, and tubes running out of her chest. Bandages and tape covered her chest; otherwise she was naked.

She was never a more Pitiful Pearl. As I looked at her lying there unconscious, it was hard not to think of all my hopes and dreams for a healthy little girl; it was hard not to feel very sad seeing her this way. But she was recovering; she would live to throw her Big Bird out of another car window or train at the zoo.

As I stood at Jennifer's bedside watching her frail, bloody body, I desperately wanted to do something for her. The only thing I could do was wash her face with a washcloth. Then I noticed that her toenails badly needed trimming. I asked the nurses for clippers, and they looked at me perplexed. Someone finally found the clippers, and I rushed to Jennifer to begin work.

It was as though Jennifer wouldn't survive if I didn't do this little act. I think my mind had snapped.

I began to sob and cry. I prayed that Jennifer somehow could sense my love for her.

Jennifer recovered quickly. She walked just two days after the operation and was released one week later. Another obstacle apparently had been hurdled. Prior to the surgery, whenever Jennifer had a serious infection or dental work, her doctors always expressed concern that some germ would get into her bloodstream, collect around her valve, and damage her heart even more. I hoped the patch job would reduce this problem.

While Jennifer was in the hospital, Rainelle and I spent lots of time in the intensive care waiting room. We saw many families with seriously ill children. Families came to Children's Hospital from all over the Midwest. Because their homes were hundreds of miles away, some of the families slept on make-shift cots in the waiting room.

We shared our stories, and I marveled at what people could endure. The newborn baby of one family had multiple heart defects, more than the surgeons could repair. The infant lost life slowly over several days.

I was aware that I didn't know what to say to these people. Worse, I didn't want to say anything, as if they were lepers who might jinx my own child. I began to understand, if not forgive, the reactions to Jennifer by other parents outside the hospital. For the moment, I was glad that I wasn't the surgeon who had to tell these parents about the imminent death of their baby.

Rainelle and I passed the time talking and practicing signs with Mrs. Busch, who regularly came to see Jennifer. Some parents in the room read inspirational books to help them cope with their troubles. Their belief in God was a great comfort to them. I often wished I could depend on my faith as they did.

One afternoon while Jennifer was recovering, a minister came to the hospital and asked about her.

"Fine," I said. "She's doing fine."

I tried to be polite, though in truth I didn't want to talk to anyone. The next question was predictable. Ministers always want to know if they can help in some way. I've never figured out just what they have in mind, but it's a nice gesture.

"Is there anything I can get for you?" he asked.

It flashed across my mind, and though I didn't say it, I wanted to: "Grapes," I thought. "I'd like some grapes."

Instead, I thanked him kindly and said I just couldn't think of a thing.

Hospitals do funny things to me.

Jennifer got ready to return to school that fall. It was September 1980. She wasn't at all upset about returning to school; in fact, she seemed excited about seeing her friends. I guessed that, after heart surgery, any activity was an improvement for her. Nevertheless, I dreaded her going back to school. She always handles the parting much better than I do.

Rainelle and I took her to the school in Olathe and got her settled in the dormitory. I started to get all misty as I walked back to the car to drive home. The feeling of missing her settled over me like a five-day rain.

There is a kind of peace for me in autumn, in spite of my hay fever. I feel a slowing down in anticipation of winter. In Kansas the prairie grasses die, and the trees, fewer than in Missouri, are all the more precious as the leaves lose their green and turn to brown.

Rainelle was still living in Missouri, I in Kansas, as we had been for the last two years. She finally got word in fall 1980 that she had successfully completed law school. Though I was happy for her, I didn't want to share in her achievement as a husband would. Except for our love for Jennifer, we led separate lives. We agreed to divorce, which was final in November.

149

Many people mistakenly think of divorce as a legal action. It is really an emotional process. Rainelle and I had been in the process of divorcing for years, though we hadn't necessarily verbalized it. With a handicapped child in the family, the process is epecially complicated; extra cooperation is required to care for the child's needs, both physical and emotional.

Rainelle and I arranged joint custody; we would share the responsibility and joy of watching Jennifer grow up.

Growing up is exactly what she began to do. After her surgery, Jennifer began to gain weight and to develop in the places one expects a young girl to develop. I watched my baby become a girl, and I wished that her progress would slow down. There probably isn't anything more normal between a father and daughter than that.

Jennifer's emotional progress was good too. Even her TV tastes were changing, moving from pure fantasy to slapstick. She watched cartoons less, preferring instead to see the Three Stooges or old Marx Brothers movies. She liked to mimic Groucho stooping over and tapping the ashes off an imaginary cigar. In fact, Jennifer likes all the old-time comics—Abbott and Costello, Laurel and Hardy—and likes to play-act them. I thought it was the slapstick element that appealed to her. But then she began writing Bob Hope's name on her papers. It is a mystery how she figured out to put Bob Hope in her group of "funny gentlemen," which is the literal translation of her sign for *comedian.*

She also continued to be something of a comedian herself, sometimes unwittingly. One day a friend and I took Jennifer to a restaurant where the parking lot had two spaces for vehicles owned by the handicapped. Jennifer saw the wheelchair symbol marking the spaces and wanted to know what it meant.

"That's for people in wheelchairs," I explained.

Her eyes lit up. Jennifer is fascinated with people in wheelchairs.

"Can't walk, can't walk," she signed.

In the restaurant Jennifer chose a table looking out over the handicapped parking. Each time a car came into the lot, Jennifer stood in anticipation, waving her arms to motion the people into the spaces. As cars continually passed by the designated spaces, she slumped in her chair, her disappointment growing. She wanted to see a wheelchair so badly. But the handicapped people didn't come to eat that night.

Finally it was too much. She snorted her disappointment and snapped her finger as if to say "phooey."

Just before Jennifer's heart surgery, we went to my cousin Bill's farm where Jennifer selected her first pet from a litter of blonde Labrador retrievers. We tied a red ribbon around his neck and watched him frolic with his brothers and sisters before taking him to his new home. Jennifer was excited. So was I.

We named him Baba, as in Baa, Baa, Black Sheep, because Jennifer can easily fingerspell and sort of vocalize that. I taught Baba to respond to sign commands (sit, come, stay, etc.) as a surprise for Jennifer. When I showed Jennifer her puppy's tricks, she was elated and put him through his paces.

She seemed to enjoy talking to her pet but didn't understand that his language skills were more limited than her own. I looked out in the backyard one Saturday afternoon and saw Jennifer asking Baba if he wanted a drink of water.

As winter settled in, Jennifer continued to do well in school. Her curriculum now included "pre-vocational activities," which means shop to most of us. Jennifer made a lamp and seemed to enjoy working with her hands.

It was hard to accept that my child at age eleven was being shunted into vocational training to program her for productive work in her adult life. But I didn't know what else to recommend. Decisions have to be made on the basis of Jennifer's capabilities as seen at the moment.

There is no Solomon to look into the future for us. The hope is that these decisions will not underestimate her abilities and unnecessarily limit her future choices.

Psychological Test Report, 3/81
Jennifer Harris, age 11 years, 3 months

Jennifer's overall obtained score (65) on the WISC-R Performance is somewhat misleading. Though it is within the Mentally Deficient range, on examination of individual subtest scores, it is found that this score is attributable chiefly to her extremely poor performance on the Picture Arrangement subtest. Her performance on this task indicates limitations in sequencing ability, and may further indicate some limitations in the area of social judgment. Though her teacher indicated that Jennifer has made rather significant progress this year in being able to interact with the other two children in her specialized classroom, imaginary friends still occupy some of Jennifer's attention at times. Some such behavior was noted during the evaluation, when Jennifer was observed to talk with first her left and then her right hand. Her teacher commented that Jennifer has specific names for each hand and refers to them as such when she so interacts. Such autistic mannerisms indicate that, very likely, emotional atypicalness enters into her test score responses, and may be a factor in accounting for the variation in her tests over the past years.

As spring approached, Jennifer's fantasy life seemed to increase. Her "finger friends" sometimes got into fights with each other. The boy, named Oiny by Jennifer, sometimes literally hit her and made her cry. The girl, named Oiry, seemed to be the gentle, happy member of the pair.

I was at a loss to know what to do. Should I encourage this fantasy? Tell Jennifer to stop? Slap her hands? Ignore it all? Sometimes Jennifer was so intent on her friends that I couldn't get her attention. She ignored my tapping on her shoulder, and her eyes appeared glazed when I tried to make eye contact.

A psychologist friend suggested that the boy and girl might represent Jennifer's sexual maturation and identity.

152

The girl was the obvious feminine development; the boy represented forbidden, angry impulses that she projected onto her hands. It was a nice theory, but I didn't know quite what to do with it.

Jennifer drew pictures of Oiny and Oiry (pages 154 and 155). She told me that she also had dreams about them. In many pictures they seemed a happy couple.

Jennifer by this time had also taken an interest in a real boy. She came home one weekend from school and said she was going to marry him. We thumbed through her school yearbook to find a picture of the lucky fellow. I hoped they wouldn't elope just yet. Why, I didn't know the slightest thing about this boy!

Jennifer's finger friends still came to play with her. But I decided that since nobody told me to get rid of my imaginary alligator when I was a kid, I wasn't going to say much about Jennifer's little people as long as they behaved.

Jennifer's recurring orthopedic problems became more pronounced as summer approached. She walked on her toes rather than striking her heels first, and she could barely walk up steps. Her increased weight—twenty-five pounds since her heart surgery—seemed to make the problem worse. I wanted her evaluated by physical therapists, but they couldn't help until the family physician made a referral. That was arranged. Jennifer then went to physical therapy for a few weeks, but the therapists recommended that an orthopedic doctor have a look. We made an appointment with an orthopedic physician who worked with kids.

As we walked into the examining room, I dreaded what he might say—special shoes, braces, even surgery.

He took Jennifer's shoes off and sighed. "I'm afraid she'll have to have surgery," he said. "Her arches are far too high, and she is having to walk on her toes."

Oiny and Oiry (1981)

The happy couple (1981)

"If it's summer, it must be surgery," I mumbled, feeling sorry that Jennifer had to endure this one more time.

Rainelle and I carefully explained to Jennifer that this time she would have an operation on her feet and that she would wear casts for three weeks. Jennifer acted compliant, almost unconcerned. She'd had so many such experiences that perhaps now it was commonplace and no cause for alarm.

On the day of the surgery, we checked Jennifer into the hospital. The nurses took a blood sample, a procedure Jennifer thoroughly hated. Everything else was routine. I decided to try to explain the operation to her once again, just to be sure she knew what to expect.

"Jennifer," I signed, "the doctor will operate on your feet. First, he will give you a shot and make you sleep so it won't hurt. He will put casts on your legs, and you will wear them for three weeks. The operation will help you walk better."

Jennifer nodded as though she understood, and I felt relieved to think she understood this operation was being done for her good.

A few minutes later I was getting ready to leave the hospital room and let her sleep for the night. She vocalized "mma, mma" to get my attention. When I looked, she began to sign, "Doctor cut off feet. Right. Can't walk, can't walk."

Her worried brow matched the questioning in her round blue eyes.

"No, no, no," I signed. "You can walk. The doctor will fix your feet. Better, better, better."

It hurt to think that Jennifer lived with this fear, but I didn't know how to relieve her of it.

The surgery went well. When Jennifer woke up in the recovery room, she looked at her feet, found they were still attached, and smiled. Rainelle patted Jennifer, who drifted back to sleep.

I hoped she would dream about running in the park with Baba.

The new school year started. Jennifer approached her twelfth birthday.

Rainelle called me one evening to talk about Jennifer and to explain a note she had sent me in the mail. It was a list of expenses for Jennifer that we had agreed to split:

Jennifer's glasses $86.00
Shoes   20.00
Wear and tear on mother   1,000,000,000.00

I immediately returned her bill with one of my own:

Doctor's bills $50.00
Allowance at school   7.00
Puppy food   1,143.00 (chalk this
                                                   off to bad
                                                   judgment)

The teasing between Rainelle and me was a good sign that our divorce had not been fatal. We worked hard to come to agreements about raising Jennifer. Rainelle was worried about the change of teachers in Jennifer's classroom. Jennifer's new teacher was inexperienced, but she was interested and dedicated. So we decided to wait and see how Jennifer got along.

Rainelle and I still had our disagreements about Jennifer, especially about her capabilities. Rainelle, for example, was concerned that Jennifer would some day read my diary and feel responsible for the breakup of her mother and father's marriage. Besides the fact that I didn't feel that way, I said that, unfortunately, there wasn't much chance that Jennifer would ever be able to read that well or even understand the events that had transpired.

On some things, however, Rainelle and I were in full agreement. Our daughter was growing and maturing beyond all expectations. She was developing into a delightful, pretty little girl with a knack for doing the unexpected.

Rainelle was also doing good things for herself. As many people do after a divorce, she lost a few pounds and began taking better care of her health. She seemed to re-establish a network of friends—a need that had been neglected in the isolation of our marriage and earlier years with raising Jennifer.

She started work part-time on a master's degree in business, with a long-range goal of getting into hospital administration. With a law degree and a business degree, she ought to be superb. I imagine our experiences with hospitals have made an impact on Rainelle, though she's never told me that was her motivation for wanting this kind of work. I think she has seen some things she'd like to change in the way hospitals work.

Meanwhile, Rainelle was having trouble finding a job. She eventually got a position with the state of Missouri as an employment discrimination complaints examiner. She wasn't excited about the salary but she seemed to relish the work.

"I feel like I'm doing at least a little bit of good for somebody," she said. "Some of the complaints aren't very well-founded, but some of the things that happen to people are outrageous."

She went on to tell me about a large settlement she had won for a client. I was happy that she was pleased with herself and her work. She seemed to be in control of her own destiny.

One night I reflected on what Jennifer's future might hold. I wondered what she would be like at age thirty or forty. I prayed that she would have a dignified existence with meaning and purpose. I wished I could guarantee that she would always have loved ones when her mother and I are gone. Despite all the problems of the past, Rainelle, Jennifer, and I have lives to live. We are more similar to than different from any other family that must regroup and plan for the future.

Jennifer's ears were broken, but our hearts were only wounded. And time heals.

CHAPTER 11

In a workshop I attended three years ago, an administrator of a school for handicapped children remarked that parents seldom truly accept their child's condition. He said parents don't accept that their handicapped children will grow up to be handicapped adults; consequently, parents don't learn about the lives of handicapped adults. His tone was critical of parents; he indicated that parents ought to be doing more. He complained that parents and relatives delude themselves deep down inside that somehow the problem will go away or will be fixed by some magic.

There is some truth in this assertion. For example, my mother once told me of a vivid dream in which Jennifer talked to her. Our dreams sometimes reveal the reality we want to exist and will try to create if it doesn't. My other friends and relatives tell me similar stories. I wish I had a hug from Jennifer for every time someone has tried to reassure me by saying, "I'll just bet the scientists will soon discover a way to operate and fix her ears." My father sends me clippings from magazines about advances in hearing aids, though Jennifer doesn't wear one. There is always hope.

Mary, a friend of mine, has taken the trouble to learn sign language. In a short time she learned to sign nearly as well as I do, and she gets along beautifully with Jennifer. Mary too has dreamed of Jennifer talking, a dream that upon waking could not be specifically remembered except for a powerful feeling that it really happened. I frequently am confronted with these fantasies by others, and it puts me on an emotional roller coaster. I wish Jennifer could hear and talk, but I know that she can't. Most important, I realize that if she could talk and had no other troubles, Jennifer would not be the same Jennifer I have come to love. If Jennifer were magically restored to normality, I would lose my little girl.

There is no doubt in my mind, however, that if a miracle surgery were made available I would want it for Jennifer. I wish she had not been born with all the problems she has had. But I am proud of what Jennifer has become. I am not embarrassed that she can't talk. Though people often stare at us, I enjoy signing with her. I would want Jennifer to be "normal" if that were possible, but I also love her as she is.

What does it mean to accept a child's handicap? When we say a person accepts a fact, a reality, do we mean intellectually or emotionally? If we "accept" the truth, does that mean we must also like what it implies, or that we are emotionally at peace with it? Can people accept something at one level of personality but not another? If we accept something at one moment, must we also accept it a moment later, or can we change from day to day, from mood to mood? Can we accept a person but not a handicap?

Guilt no doubt complicates the task of acceptance. I am (as is Rainelle) responsible for Jennifer's existence. It is hard not to blame myself for her handicaps, and it is hard not to shift the blame to someone else. I sometimes wondered if Jennifer was being punished for my sins or for her own in a former life. When Rainelle and I began to understand that Jennifer may have been affected by rubella in pregnancy, we were surprised.

"Did you know you had measles?" I asked.

"No, I remember I had a kidney infection, but no measles," Rainelle said.

"Well, I guess we should have paid more attention," I said.

There was a feeling of opportunity lost. All the problems might have been easily avoided.

Professionals themselves often blame parents, directly or indirectly, for the child's handicaps. For example, popular theories of autism hold that "refrigerator mothers," cold and aloof, cause children to be autistic. I have been in graduate classes and training seminars in which the lecturer stated that all emotional problems in children are caused by dysfunctional parents. One famous therapist calls this the "hate the parents syndrome." Though these kinds of simplistic statements make me angry, they also raise self-doubt. I wonder if I'm still doing something that impedes Jennifer's progress.

The worst part is that professionals in practice will seldom acknowledge these beliefs directly. Instead, a raised eyebrow or probing question is the giveaway. Once, when Jennifer needed help with toilet training, a psychologist evaluating her asked what kind of stresses there were at home between Rainelle and me. I said I didn't think Jennifer's toilet training problems were related to other problems at home; but perhaps I was just being defensive.

Rainelle and I spent years searching for the cause of Jennifer's troubles. We saw physicians, psychologists, neurologists, and audiologists, hoping to find an answer. Would the answer have been so important if we hadn't thought locating the cause would relieve us of blame? Many professionals, however, told us to quit looking for the answer, because it didn't matter. As one audiologist at the Kansas University Medical Center said, "It's academic." I was grateful for this commonsense approach, one which seemed to dismiss the importance of finding a responsible agent.

Unfortunately, we may also have thought that giving up the quest for a full explanation was tantamount to

161

"accepting" that Jennifer would forever be handicapped. Without knowing the cause, how could there be a cure? In this way disabilities that are fully "acceptable" to us as parents, emotionally and intellectually, can never be transformed through effort and care. Yet it would seem to be loving for parents to be realistic and "accept" their child's handicap. The paradox is that doing so may lead to complacency and resignation.

Rainelle was once accused by a psychologist of being "unrealistic" about Jennifer's handicaps. But perhaps it was this unrealistic attitude, this rejection of the probable, that created hope and provided energy for working with Jennifer. It may also be true that Rainelle's continued hope and her unwillingness to accept "reality" was a source of disagreement between her and me. I suppose it could be said that while Rainelle was always hoping for the best, I was always preparing for the worst.

In some cases, significant change in the child never happens. But we do not know in advance when hope and patience and care will make a difference. Meanwhile, some parents will go on not accepting their child's handicap. Deep down, the part of us not coldly logical and rational still believes in the possibility of transformation.

Every so often, people need to sit down and take stock of their lives and situations. Things need to be re-evaluated and reconsidered. Sometimes you learn something that might change your ideas and attitudes. Sometimes things change and the old ways of thinking don't fit any more.

But when a change occurs before the last one has had time to sink in, it is difficult to sort everything out. That is the problem we faced raising Jennifer until about 1980. First one handicap, then another was discovered, leaving inadequate time to comprehend the implications. If all of Jennifer's problems had been apparent at birth, the shock might have been different. But Rainelle and I reeled like punch-drunk sailors as Jennifer's problems were revealed at intervals spaced just far enough apart to keep us unbalanced. How could we accept a handicap and its implications when we didn't realize it existed because it was not yet apparent?

The ripple effects from Jennifer's various handicaps discovered years earlier are still coming to shore. Perhaps the major changes in my life are slowing down enough to allow my mind to feel the waves lap at consciousness. For example, Rainelle and I had known for years that Jennifer's feet were not normal. After all, Jennifer wore special shoes when she was six. But we otherwise ignored her feet until Mary mentioned them in 1981.

"I don't know how she can walk at all on those feet," Mary said.

Indeed, Jennifer was having difficulty walking. I had attributed the problem not to her feet, however, but to her rapid growth. After some persuasion by Mary, I reluctantly agreed to have Jennifer's feet examined.

But why did I then take her to a physical therapist instead of an orthopedic doctor? Did I really think the right exercise would cure misshapened feet? Or did I unconsciously want to avoid the reality that Jennifer might have another serious defect? It just takes a long time, years in fact, for the fog of self-delusion or confusion to be lifted. One seldom understands the extent of confusion until it has been lifted. How many more awakenings will there be for me?

To raise a handicapped child is to be lost in a blanket of fog with your entire family. Each member of the family is lost in a different place. As you wander around trying to find each other, you walk in circles. If you walk into a relatively clear area, you think you can see again and you breathe a sigh of relief. But soon the wind changes and you are once more groping in a patch of fog. You call out to members of your family, but they too are unable to get oriented.

A year ago I thought I could see clearly what my family had not yet been able to see. At a holiday dinner, my sister approached me.

"Jennifer used her voice and said a word to me!" she said excitedly.

"Oh?" I said, reluctant to say more and tell Susan that she could not see through the fog.

Sometimes it is tempting to walk back into the fog with your family. After all, my sister has a bond with Jennifer that I've never been able to explain considering the small amount of time they've actually spent together. Jennifer has always allowed Susan to comb her hair or put makeup on her. Jennifer goes to Susan and gives her hugs and kisses when no one else in the room (including me) gets so much as a nod of recognition. If Jennifer were to talk to anyone, she would talk to Susan.

I desperately wanted to believe Susan, but I knew it just wasn't true. Jennifer can't hear and can't talk. She never will.

Do I accept Jennifer more or accept her less if I succumb to the temptation to believe she can talk, or may someday talk? Certainly there was and is a force, a pressure to be reconciled with the beliefs of Rainelle and my family about Jennifer's condition. But who among us accepts Jennifer more—those who love this child so much that they cannot believe there will be no magical fix for her problems? Or those who think they see the future a bit more clearly, however temporarily, by having wandered into a clearing in the fog? Who would even dare attempt to answer such a question?

There are many reasons why parents don't actively try to learn about what futures their handicapped children may face. Though my signing is not as good as I'd like it to be, I was once complimented by a deaf educator.

"You sign well for a father," he said. "Most parents don't learn to sign at all," he added critically.

"Well, languages are hard for some people," I said. "Besides, you have to realize that learning to sign is an admission that your child can't talk and probably never will learn well enough to communicate in the hearing world. That's hard for parents to accept."

"But if they can't sign, they can't participate in their child's life, their child's future," he said.

"True, but as unfortunate as that is, you have to understand that looking at the future may not be very pleasant," I said. "The more severe the handicap, the more likely we are to avoid the implications."

Sometimes I also don't want to think any more about the lives of handicapped adults. I want to forget what awareness I already have. Besides having Jennifer, I've worked in vocational rehabilitation and in jails; I've seen more depressing human tragedy than I really want to remember.

Some of my clients lead very marginal existences. One lady I knew was picked up by the police for loitering under a bridge. She had been living there, eating tins of cat food to stay alive. I've worked with remarkably intelligent blind people who were unable to find work more challenging than answering phones. The lives of handicapped adults are not easy. Maybe that's why parents don't want to learn more about them. It is too painful.

On the other hand, when I start to rant and rave about the lives of handicapped adults, many people—professionals included—smile knowingly and hint that I'm too close to these problems. Too much denial or too much awareness. Either way it can be a problem. It is hard to maintain balance.

What upsets me most is that people with handicaps are so often denied their dignity. In a sheltered workshop where I used to work, the workers had to use an elevator to get from one floor to the next. Many of them had cerebral palsy or other physical ailments that impeded rapid movement. Consequently, the elevator was often stopped for long intervals while people got on and off at their own speed. It was no big problem, but movement in the building was a little slow.

165

The director of the program was a hard driver who believed everyone should learn to work and be self-sufficient. But sometimes I think he had his priorities in the wrong order. He was upset about the slow elevator, so he installed a buzzer. The buzzer went off when the elevator door stayed open more than ten seconds. I don't think he understood how embarrassing it was for people, moving as fast as they could, to be ridiculed by this impersonal reminder of their infirmities. I know I can't always protect Jennifer from such indignities.

Some attitudes about people with handicaps can be not only embarrassing but damaging. In a conversation with me once, a well-trained pyschologist used the phrase "deaf and dumb." Old myths die hard. I'm not surprised when untrained people say such things. But imagine the damage a professional can cause with such ignorance. That's why I worry about the quality of care Jennifer will receive when she is an adult.

I have also seen adults with handicaps who lead happy, productive lives. I took Jennifer to the Topeka deaf club. Deaf people gather there once a month to socialize. Though I couldn't follow their rapid signing in the business meeting, I enjoyed playing cards and trying to communicate with them. They patiently corrected my signs and seemed to like Jennifer. But I wonder if Jennifer will be welcome by herself in such a club when she is an adult. She is in a special education classroom at the school for the deaf and is already out of the mainstream of her deaf peers. But perhaps I anticipate problems that will never occur or be an issue. Maybe Jennifer won't want to go to the club. She will exercise her own choices.

Though I may not be so optimistic as to believe, even unconsciously, that Jennifer will one day have hearing and normal intelligence and coping skills, I am not without hope for a happy future for her.

Some of my musings about Jennifer's future are fun to think about. Frequently I have wondered what the man who might marry Jennifer would be like. I picture Jennifer's suitor looking much like her. I laugh to myself when I visualize him asking for her hand in sign language.

Then I think that, of course, it would be out of character for Jennifer to do anything but elope. If Jennifer grows up to be capable of pulling off an elopement, I'll be very happy. But you can be sure that I won't say that to her.

One night several years ago I had a dream: Jennifer is walking alone down a sidewalk, effortlessly and happily dragging her suitcase. Opening two swinging doors, she enters a hotel lobby and wordlessly leaves her suitcase at the feet of a bellboy who, without question, picks up the bag and follows Jennifer to the front desk. Behind the desk are several adults and one male child about Jennifer's age. He approaches Jennifer and both smile. She silently gestures toward the keys and he, seeming to understand intuitively, reaches for a room key before placing a registration card and pen before her. She scrawls her name in childish script, the last several letters trailing off the card. She then pulls out two pennies and lays them confidently on the desk.

She turns and walks away, having completed her transaction successfully without a word said. Her life continues.

Of course, there remain more immediate and mundane concerns about Jennifer. After her foot surgery in the summer of 1981, I thought her foot problems would be much improved. But the surgeon said then that Jennifer still needed surgery on her toes, perhaps the next summer. She was limping very badly, and I was concerned.

[Diary, October 1981]

> Warts. Warts. First, feet that look like two cocked bows without arrows. Now, warts. I thought she was limping because her foot surgery had failed, had made her feet worse than before. Oh, I felt sad. But now, a friend noticed the warts. So I called the orthopedic surgeon. He said he doesn't do warts. Specialist, you know. But it's only warts, and they'll come off. Please, let that be all. Let her walk without pain.

[Two weeks later]

Oh, boy! The wart surgery was a success. The family doctor burned them off with an electric needle. He said he could do only one foot at a time, so Rainelle twice took Jennifer to the doctor's office. The first time Jennifer was told what the doctor would do, and she cooperated. But she didn't like it. Rainelle said she explained to Jennifer that the doctor would work on the other foot next week. Jennifer said no, the other foot was fine and that the doctor would look at it and say okay. Rainelle and Jennifer argued. Rainelle did not want Jennifer to get her hopes up and expect no more pain.

The day came for the second appointment. I hadn't seen Jennifer between appointments. Rainelle had been paying close attention to the foot already treated, which was healing nicely. Jennifer said it was better, and repeated that the other foot was fine too and that the doctor would look at it and say so. Rainelle told Jennifer, no, the doctor would probably have to fix that foot also.

In the office, the doctor had Jennifer slip her shoe and sock off of the treated foot. Yes, it looked good. Now for the other foot.

He stared in disbelief. "Didn't she have warts on this foot too?" he asked, looking at her chart.

"Yes," said Rainelle, looking at Jennifer's feet.

But the warts were gone. Jennifer started putting her shoes and socks back on, happily signing, "Finished, finished."

I think my kid willed her warts away!

She's walking much better now. In the morning when she first gets up, she's a bit stiff, but when she's happy, she fairly well struts and prances. She got a new pair of sneakers that she was proud of. They weren't Red Ball Jets like I used to wear, but the effect was similar.

Oh, to be a kid again and find magic in tennis shoes.

Oh, to be able to will away warts.

CHAPTER 12

With the school year rapidly passing and Jennifer well into her twelfth year, I find our lives developing a pleasant routine. It is fun and comforting to do normal, unremarkable things regularly with Jennifer. So much time in earlier years was spent going to doctors and schools that it was hard to find time for day-to-day living.

Now, when she comes home from school on weekends, we have everything down to a science. Friday afternoon I pick her up at 4:30. She arrives in Topeka on the school bus which leaves from her dormitory in Olathe a couple of hours earlier. Jennifer carries her grocery sack full of schoolwork to the car, and we get in. I try to get a hug and a kiss to say hello, but Jennifer hides her head in her arms and laughs.

"Food store," she signs. "Food store."

"Okay," I sign. "We'll go to the food store."

Before I start the car, I tell her I'm happy to see her. I stroke her hair. After a week, my hands are hungry to touch her; but Jennifer is impatient.

"Now food store," she signs.

"Okay, okay, food store," I reply.

Jennifer likes the grocery store because it has a magazine rack and doughnuts for a Friday afternoon treat.

169

I start the car and pull out of the parking lot. Jennifer suddenly decides she wants to tell me about her week at school. As I drive through traffic, she whacks me on the shoulder, and I'm torn between the need to drive the car safely and the desire to show Jennifer I really do care about her Valentine's day party at school. I compromise and we talk at stoplights.

Jennifer gets a *Mad* magazine from the back seat to read while I drive. If I'm ever stopped by a policeman and have to tell him I am a college professor, I hope he either has children or fails to notice the stack of comic books in the back seat of my car.

We arrive at the grocery store. We always go to the same store because its magazine rack is best situated for Jennifer to stay safely while I shop. Jennifer walks into the store with me and asks if she can go read—an act which astonishes and pleases me anew each time she repeats it. She signs, "Read," and raises her eyebrows to indicate a question. I sign, "Yes, read," to give permission, and off she goes. She sits down on the floor, absorbed in her selection, while I shop for food for the weekend.

On the way to the check-out, I stop to ask Jennifer if she likes the doughnuts I've picked. I know pretty well what she likes; once in awhile she changes her mind, though, and we have to go to the back of the store for a personal tour of the bakery. Daughters can't let daddies get too sure about things.

When money is low, I sometimes tell Jennifer she can have either her comic book or the doughnuts.

"Choose one," I say.

"Both," she signs as she closes her eyes, shakes her head, and grins.

"No, choose one," I repeat.

"Two books?" Jennifer asks, driving a hard bargain.

Occasionally, I give in and let her get two books. Daddies ought to encourage children to ask for what they want.

We exit the grocery store, stage right, but there is a

170

smoked-meat stand in our way, enticing us to buy barbecued ribs or chicken. Jennifer wants a sample. I want the whole stand. We buy ribs for later.

On the way to the car I am cautious to watch for cars because Jennifer is often careless.

"Watch for cars," I sign, but Jennifer is asking me to open the doughnuts.

On the way home, Jennifer asks about Baba the wonder dog.

"See Baba?" she signs.

"Yes," I signal and Jennifer smiles.

When we arrive home, Jennifer gets out of the car. She leaves her door open as she walks up the steps to the house. I wait for her to turn around. When I catch her attention, I tell her to come and shut the door.

"Who, me?" her expression indicates.

I give her something to carry to the house, though not much because she's not very strong or steady. I do not let her carry the doughnuts.

Inside the house, Jennifer sometimes helps put the groceries away. Occasionally the laundry soap ends up in the refrigerator. Sometimes she runs upstairs to play in her room as I fix dinner. Master chef that I am, the smoked ribs usually get served.

We while away the evening watching TV if something good is on (Charlie Brown cartoon, Laurel and Hardy, or other "funny gentlemen" movies). Jennifer frequently gets tired early and goes to bed. If she does, nine times out of ten she crawls between the sheets without changing into her pj's. Sometimes I wake her to make her change.

Saturday morning comes early. Jennifer wakes up at 7:00 and heads downstairs. She pours herself a bowl of Frosted Flakes (no milk, thank you) and turns on the TV. I lie in bed trying to ignore the reality of morning but

171

appreciating that Jennifer can now be allowed downstairs by herself. Nevertheless, I remain alert for suspicious noises.

The remainder of the morning is spent lazily. I get up, eat breakfast, read a little, and watch cartoons with Jennifer. I like Bugs Bunny.

I tell Jennifer to brush her teeth and her hair. These tasks she can do by herself. But she needs help taking a shower and washing her hair because she can't get the water turned on right. I suspect she could figure it out if she really wanted to take a shower.

In the afternoon, Jennifer asks to go to "old book store" to buy used comics. Jennifer could spend hours looking at old *Mad* magazines—and frequently does. If the weather is nice, I let her go to the park across the street to swing. Ours is not a busy street, but I tell her to look out for cars. Anxiously, I watch her as she walks across the yard then across the street. I notice whether she looks for cars. Sometimes she does; sometimes she doesn't.

I often let Baba go to the park with Jennifer, though he's no more careful of cars than she. If he spies an interesting squirrel, he tears off after it, though he's never yet caught one. In reality he's not much protection for Jennifer. But he's big and his appearance might deter someone from bothering Jennifer. Good thing squirrels can't talk.

If we're really in a good mood, Saturday evening is pizza and movie time. Jennifer likes to go to Fun-Time Pizza where they have video games and mechanical cartoon characters that sing rock songs on a stage every ten minutes or so. There is a lot of movement and color, which is good because then you don't notice the pizza. My friend Mary who goes with us says we should eat pizza elsewhere, then go to Fun-Time to let Jennifer play. That seems almost un-American to me, though I can't say why.

Sundays are much like Saturdays except the old book store is closed. Jennifer gladly substitutes a convenience store where there are new comic books. I've been more disciplined recently about trips to the convenience store. I try to have Jennifer choose between the old book store and the convenience store on any given weekend. Thus, Jennifer is learning to plan several days at once and to spread out her treats. She accepts this rationing well, though she always tries to get me to change my mind.

Sometime during the weekend I look through Jennifer's schoolwork. If there is something unusual I try to get her to talk to me about it, but she's seldom interested. She'd rather sit at the table and draw pictures or write.

I frequently talk with Rainelle by phone on weekends. We laugh at the funny things Jennifer has done recently and talk about any problems she is having at school. Jennifer seems to enjoy being with her mother and with me and wants to know whose house she'll go to the next weekend. Having three homes (the dormitory at school and two parent's places) doesn't seem to be a major problem. I tell Jennifer I am talking to Rainelle on the phone, so she knows we stay up to date on her behavior.

Sometimes I also learn some amazing things about Jennifer by talking with Rainelle. One event that I thought Jennifer had not understood came up when she was with Rainelle. Rainelle and I discussed it later and marveled that Jennifer had, in fact, understood.

It was the Christmas season, 1981. Jennifer and I went to visit my brother in St. Louis. We had a nice visit. On the way back I decided to drive through Columbia, Missouri, where Jennifer was born. I enjoy driving through the town, when time allows, to see how it has changed and to visit the campus where I did my undergraduate study.

First we drove through the trailer court where we lived for three years. I asked Jennifer if she remembered it. She nodded her head yes, but I couldn't sense any

173

spark of excitement in her recognition. When I told her we had lived there, she opened a comic book to read.

The university hospital where Jennifer was born is just over the hill from the trailer court. Her first heart surgery was done there. The Pee Wee program she attended was in a building next to the main hospital. As we drove into view of the site, a cascade of memories washed over me; but I wondered if Jennifer remembered.

"That's the hospital where you were born," I signed and pointed to the top floors of the building. "Do you remember?"

Jennifer looked mildly interested and said she remembered, but I still wasn't sure.

I told her she was a little baby when she was there.

"Finish, past, growing now," Jennifer signed.

I agreed and asked her if she wanted to go eat, an idea she enthusiastically endorsed.

It wasn't until Jennifer saw Rainelle that she talked again about the visit to Columbia. She told Rainelle she had seen the hospital where she was born. She said she was a baby then, but was a big girl now. Jennifer talked about the visit briefly, then went on to play and read her books.

Rainelle and I were tickled that Jennifer remembered and showed some interest in and understanding of her origins. But she isn't preoccupied with her past. She appears to be more interested in what she is doing now and what she could do next. She is interested in comic books, food, cartoons, dinosaur bones, "funny gentlemen," parties, vacations, and growing up. She has lots to do.

Her choice to acknowledge but not to live in the past seems altogether wise. It is a decision that seems sensible for me to follow as well when memories crowd their way to the surface.

This book was typeset in 11/13 Times Roman by Harlowe Typography Inc., of Brentwood, Maryland. It was printed on 60 lb. Lakewood by BookCrafters, Inc., of Chelsea, Michigan. The text was designed by Meryl Goodman Thomas. The cover was designed by Lisa Ann Feldman.